VOL. 4

DIGESTIVE SYSTEM & METABOLISM

wonders of the
HUMAN
BODY

Dr. Tommy Mitchell

First printing: August 2018

Master Books® is a division of the New Leaf Publishing Group, Inc.

ISBN: 978-1-68344-069-7
ISBN: 978-1-61458-672-2 (digital)
Library of Congress Number: 2018949551

Cover by Diana Bogardus
Interior by Jennifer Bauer

Unless otherwise noted, Scripture quotations are from the New King James Version of the Bible.

Please consider requesting that a copy of this volume be purchased by your local library system.

Printed in the United States

Please visit our website for other great titles:
www.masterbooks.com

For information regarding author interviews, please contact the publicity department at (870) 438-5288.

Master Books®
A Division of New Leaf Publishing Group
www.masterbooks.com

Dedication
For Mack and Marilyn Locklear,
True Heroes of the Faith

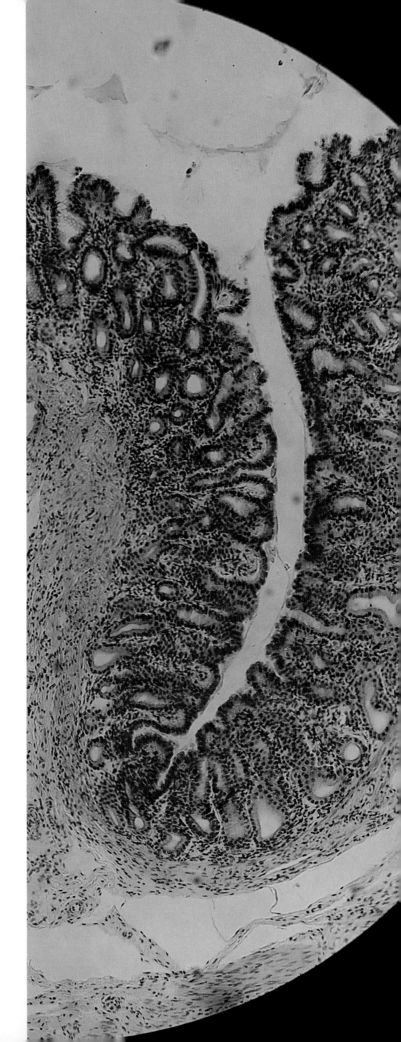

TABLE OF CONTENTS

INTRODUCTION

Here is a simple fact. Our bodies need energy.

Without a constant supply of energy, we could not think because our brains would not function. We could not walk because our muscles would not contract. We could not . . . well, you get the idea.

Where does all this energy come from? It comes from the food we take in!

Our bodies also need raw materials to repair a bone when it is broken and even to build up stronger muscles when we exercise. These raw materials come from the food we eat.

So how does the cereal you had for breakfast become energy? Or the popcorn you had at the ballgame? How does the chicken you had for supper provide the amino acids the body needs to build proteins? These are the things we will examine in depth in this volume of *Wonders of the Human Body*.

Welcome to our exploration of the digestive system!

What is Digestion?

At first glance, this may seem like a simple question. After all, we use the terms "digest" and "digestion" almost every day. But what do these words really mean?

Digestion is the process by which the food we take in is converted to substances needed by our bodies. Those substances may then serve as fuel from which energy is obtained or raw materials, which are building blocks for more complex molecules or structures. After all, the foods we eat are made up of very complex substances, aren't they? An undigested carrot is of little use to the body. However, when the carrot is broken down into its much simpler components, it becomes very useful indeed. The same is true of the other things we eat. Yes, even Brussels sprouts can be broken down into things the body needs.

Think of it this way. The gasoline that we put into a car is used to power the car's engine. The gasoline is already in a form that the car can directly burn to produce energy. This fuel is burned in the engine to make the car go. The gasoline does not need to be broken down (in a sense, digested) to be useful. It is used "as is."

Food is different. It must be broken down into more useful forms before it can be used by our bodies, either as fuel or raw material. It must be digested.

But things don't end there. The substances that result from the breakdown of food must then be absorbed into the bloodstream to then be utilized by the body. You will soon understand how all this takes place!

Man is a Special Creation

As with all our explorations into the complexity of the human body, when you see the incredible design of the digestive system, you ultimately have to ask yourself, "Can this all possibly be an accident? Something that happened by chance?" The answer is obviously a resounding, "No!"

We are not the product of evolution. We are not animals. Man is a special creation.

Then God said, "Let Us make man in Our image,
according to Our likeness;
let them have dominion over the fish of the sea,
over the birds of the air, and over the cattle,
over all the earth and over every creeping thing
that creeps on the earth."
So God created man in His own image;
in the image of God He created him;
male and female He created them.

(Genesis 1:26–27)

May we continually acknowledge God our Creator as we proceed though our study.

OVERVIEW OF THE DIGESTIVE SYSTEM

The digestive system is composed of two groups of organs — the gastrointestinal (GI) tract and the accessory digestive organs.

The gastrointestinal tract, also known as the alimentary canal, is a long tube that extends from the mouth to the anus. Contraction of the muscles in this tube propels food along its journey from beginning to end. The GI tract is comprised of the mouth, pharynx, esophagus, stomach, small intestine, and large intestine. It is about 20–24 feet long in the average person.

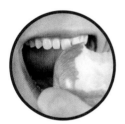 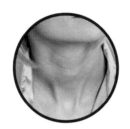  

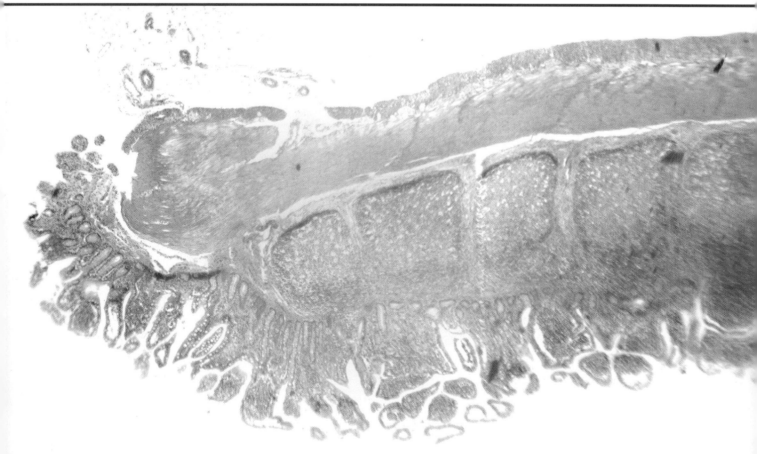

Microscopic section of the large intestine

The processes of digestion and absorption both take place in the GI tract. Interestingly, because the GI tract is open to the outside at both ends, food passing through it is technically not ever inside the body. Only the breakdown products from the digestion of food ever cross through the GI tract's walls to enter the body.

The accessory digestive organs are the teeth, tongue, salivary glands, liver, gallbladder, and pancreas. The teeth and tongue are involved with chewing and swallowing. These are the only accessory digestive organs that come into contact with the food. The remaining four accessory organs function by producing and/or delivering secretions that assist in the digestion and absorption of food.

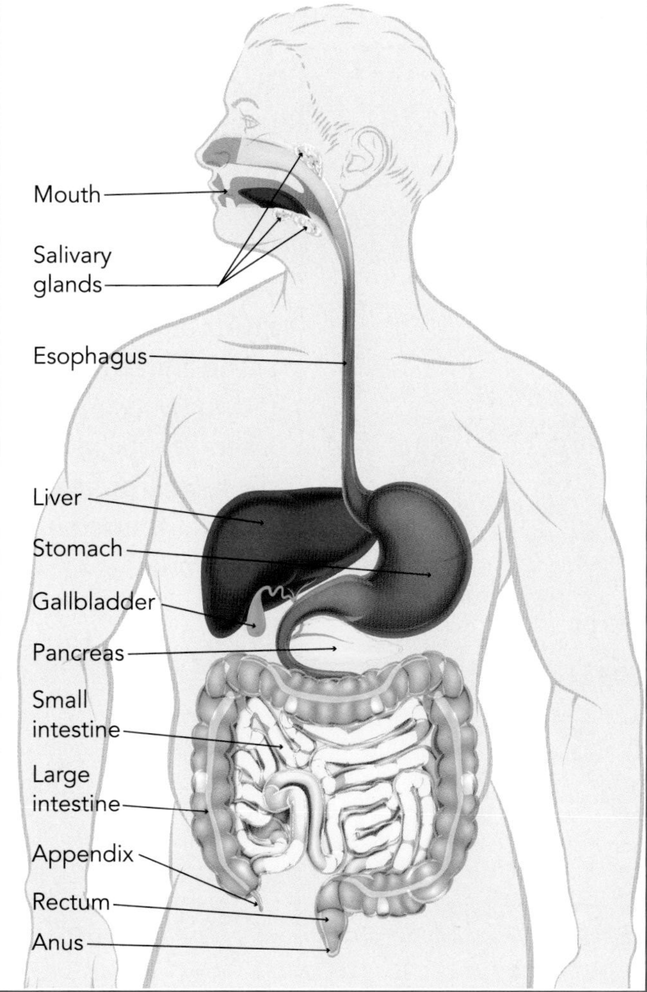

Major Functions of the Digestive System

Even though the GI tract is, in one sense at least, simply a long tube, it performs remarkable functions. Our Creator designed the GI tract to carry out a complex set of activities. Let us examine the basic processes of the digestive system more closely.

The first function of the digestive system is called *ingestion*. No surprise here, right? This simply means taking food into the GI tract. Eating and drinking is ingestion.

The next function of the digestive system is *propulsion*. That is, the food is moved along the length of the GI tract. The muscular walls of the GI tract squeeze and relax in a process called *peristalsis*. As this muscle activity occurs, not only is food propelled along, but some mixing and grinding of the food also takes place.

TAKING A CLOSER LOOK
The Digestive System

Mouth

Salivary glands

Esophagus

Liver

Stomach

Gallbladder

Pancreas

Small intestine

Large intestine

Appendix

Rectum

Anus

TAKING A CLOSER LOOK
Peristalsis

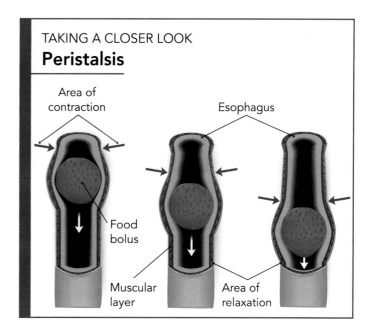

Area of contraction

Esophagus

Food bolus

Muscular layer

Area of relaxation

Next, there is the process of *digestion*, and it has two components. First, there is *mechanical digestion,* which is the physical breaking down of food into smaller pieces. This includes the tearing and grinding of food by the teeth, and the churning of food in the stomach. Then, there is *chemical digestion*. Here, we find the various digestive enzymes breaking food down into its more basic components.

Next comes the process of *absorption*. Here, the breakdown products of chemical digestion move into the cells that line the lumen of the GI tract. From here, these substances then move into the blood stream to be used throughout the body.

The final process is *elimination*. Here, indigestible material and other substances are removed as they reach the end of the GI tract. The material eliminated is called *feces* and leaves the body through the anus.

Layers of the GI Tract

The GI tract is essentially a long tube. The wall of the tube is made of several layers. In order for you to digest your food and absorb nutrients from it, the tissues in the GI tract wall must perform a variety of functions, such as squeezing the tube's contents, secreting chemicals that help digest food, and allowing the nutrients to travel through the wall. The wall of each section of the GI tract has its own anatomical features that enable it to do its jobs. While the oral cavity and pharynx have their own unique anatomy, the remaining sections of the GI tract, from the esophagus to the anus, have walls made of the same four basic layers. Let's see how they are arranged.

If you look at a cross section of the GI tract, you will see an opening in the middle, called the *lumen*. The food you chew up and swallow enters the lumen, where it is processed and moved along from section to section. The lumen is surrounded by four layers of tissue. Starting at the lumen and moving outward, these layers are the *mucosa*, the *submucosa*, the *muscularis externa*, and the *serosa*.

TAKING A CLOSER LOOK
Tissue Layers of the GI Tract

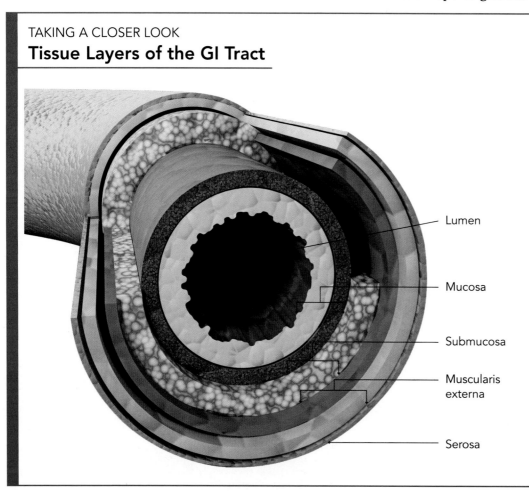

Lumen

Mucosa

Submucosa

Muscularis externa

Serosa

The Mucosa

The innermost tissue layer in the GI tract wall is called the mucosa. This layer lines the lumen of the GI tract and thus comes into contact with material passing though the digestive system. The mucosa is itself made up of three layers (wouldn't you just know it . . .).

The first is the *epithelium*. This is the layer in direct contact with the lumen. It is made up of different types of cells that perform needed functions. Some cells in the epithelium secrete mucus. This mucus not only helps food slide through the GI tract, but also helps protect the digestive organs from being damaged by the chemicals secreted to digest food.

Scattered throughout the GI tract epithelium are several specialized cell types. Some secrete chemicals and enzymes that help digest food. Others aid in absorption of the breakdown products as food is digested. We will explore many of these in depth as our study progresses.

Cells in the epithelium are replaced rapidly. They usually last about 7 days. The old cells slough off into the lumen and are carried away and eliminated in the feces.

Moving outward from the lumen, we find the *lamina propria*. This layer of connective tissue contains lots of capillaries. Blood in the capillaries brings oxygen and nutrients to the epithelial cells. These blood vessels also carry away materials absorbed from the

TAKING A CLOSER LOOK
Layers of the GI Tract

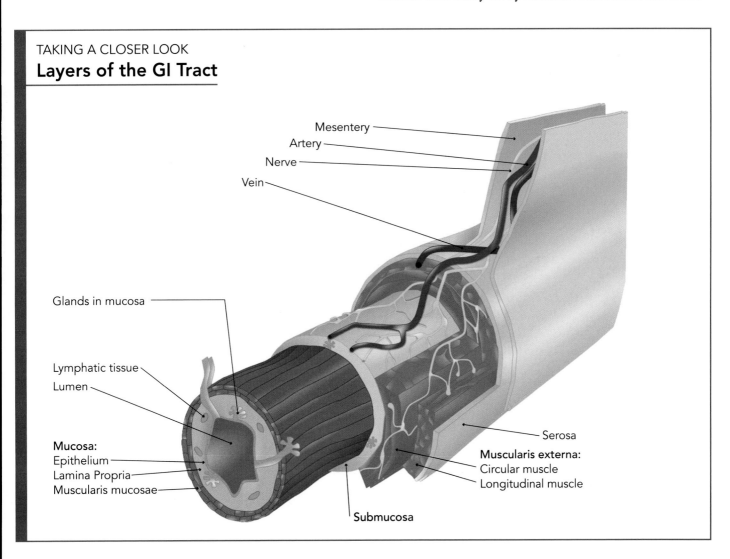

lumen as food is digested. Also found in the lamina propria are special immune system cells. These cells prevent infectious agents (bacteria, etc.) from invading the body through the walls of the GI tract.

The third layer of the mucosa is the *muscularis mucosae*. This is a tiny layer of smooth muscle fibers. These fibers allow the epithelial lining of the mucosa to expand and contract as conditions warrant. This helps regulate the surface area available for secretion and absorption. This thin muscular layer is not the only muscle found in the GI tract wall. A more robust layer of muscle is found farther out in the wall.

The Submucosa

Below the mucosa is the *submucosa*, a word that literally means "below the mucosa," just like *submarine* means "below the sea." Indeed, the submucosa provides a foundation for the mucosa.

The dense connective tissue of the submucosa supports the overlying mucosa as it expands to accommodate food to be digested and shrinks back when digestion is completed.

The blood and nerve supply of the GI tract run through this foundation. Nerve fibers regulate the GI tract's activities. The blood vessels carry away the breakdown products of food as it is absorbed. The blood vessels in the submucosa also bring oxygen and nutrients to the GI tract tissues, because the walls of the GI tract, though responsible for getting nutrients from the food we eat, are not directly supplied with those nutrients.

The Muscularis Externa

Moving farther away from the lumen, the next layer is the *muscularis externa*. This sturdy layer of muscle propels food through the GI tract.

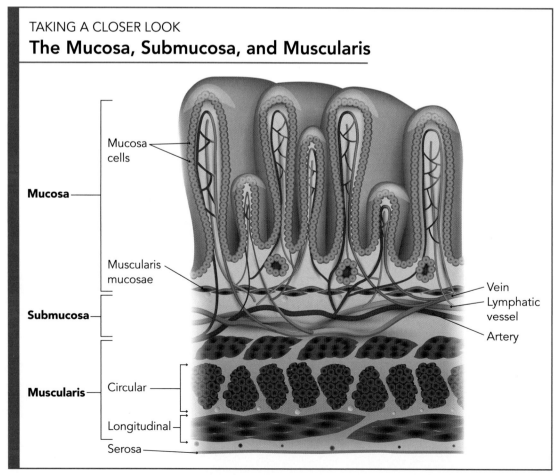

TAKING A CLOSER LOOK
The Mucosa, Submucosa, and Muscularis

Mucosa cells

Mucosa

Muscularis mucosae

Vein
Lymphatic vessel
Artery

Submucosa

Muscularis — Circular

Longitudinal

Serosa

Two different types of muscle compose the muscularis externa. Which type dominates varies from section to section. In the mouth, pharynx, and upper esophagus, as well as in the final portion of the colon, the muscles in the muscularis externa are skeletal muscle.

As you (hopefully!) recall, skeletal muscle is under voluntary conscious control. This means you can control the act of swallowing and the mechanics of elimination. It does not take much imagination to appreciate the importance of having voluntary control of these activities.

Throughout the remainder of the GI tract, the muscularis externa consists of smooth muscle, which is not under voluntary control. This is just as it should be. After all, it would be very inconvenient if you had to consciously control each step of the digestive process, thinking, "That hamburger has spent enough time being processed in this part of my small intestine and is ready to slowly move along to the next." Fortunately, you don't. Your smooth muscle responds to the instructions provided by the mechanisms that automatically monitor and regulate all the activities of the marvelous factory-like assembly line that is your GI tract.

Once again, our Master Designer has put exactly the right kinds of muscles in all the right places! Skeletal muscle where you need conscious control, smooth muscle where you don't. Sounds like the right design to me.

The Serosa

Once you swallow your food, it enters the part of the GI tract that is located in the abdominopelvic cavity, starting with the stomach. From the stomach onward, the GI tract tube is covered by a layer of connective tissue called the *serosa*. The serosa is the outermost of the layers of the GI tract, and it helps provide support for the organs of the GI tract. The serosa forms not only the outer covering for the GI tract, but at the same time acts as the slick lining that covers the contents of the abdominopelvic cavity.

The words *serosa* and *serous membrane* are related to the Latin word *serum,* which is a thin, watery fluid.

The serosa is made of connective tissue covered by a thin layer of epithelium called *mesothelium*. The epithelial tissue covering most internal organs and lining most body cavities is called mesothelium. Mesothelial cells secrete a lubricating fluid that helps organs covered by mesothelium slide past each other.

The outermost layer of the GI tract is slightly different for the esophagus. This organ resides in the thoracic cavity and lacks a full serosal covering. The esophagus, as we shall see later, is anchored in the chest cavity and doesn't need to slide past anything. The esophagus, therefore, instead of a serosa, has only a thin connective tissue layer helping hold it in place. This layer is called the *adventitia*.

The Peritoneum

The double-layered serous membrane that lines the abdominopelvic cavity is called the peritoneum. The peritoneum covers, at least partially, most of the organs in the abdomen. It also forms the innermost layer of the abdominal wall.

The peritoneal membrane, like other body cavity linings, consists of connective tissue covered by a thin layer of mesothelium. Does this sound familiar? Does this sound like the serosa we learned about earlier? You recall that the serosa — made of connective tissue covered by mesothelium — covers the outside of the GI tract. Well, the part of the peritoneum that covers the surface of the organs is called the *visceral peritoneum*. This is just another name for the serosa! They are one and the same. The other portion of the peritoneum that lines the abdominopelvic cavity just beneath the abdominal wall is called the *parietal peritoneum*.

The double-layered construction of the peritoneum is most easily understood by a simple analogy. If you take a partially inflated balloon and push your fist slowly into it, you get the idea of how the peritoneum works. Think of your fist as an organ.

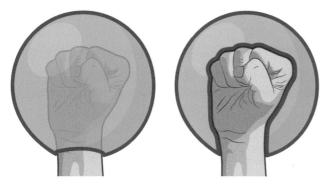

Your fist is covered tightly by a layer analogous to the *visceral peritoneum*. The other side of the balloon is analogous to the *parietal peritoneum,* the portion of the peritoneum that contacts the abdominal wall. Your peritoneum-covered fist is now inside a peritoneum-lined abdominal cavity. That's pretty much how the peritoneum works. In fact, that's pretty much how the peritoneum forms in a developing baby, long before birth when its organs are taking shape.

Remember, the reason that the peritoneum is called a serous membrane is that the cells of the mesothelium secrete a small amount of serum-like fluid to lubricate the peritoneal cavity. This lubrication allows the surfaces of organs to glide across one another easily, protecting the organs by preventing friction and snags.

Not all organs are completely surrounded by the peritoneum. Some organs are located in the very back of the abdominopelvic cavity. Only their front surfaces are covered by the peritoneum. These organs are said to be *retroperitoneal*. This word means "behind the peritoneum."

There are places where the peritoneal membrane's layers, after enveloping an organ, are actually fused together. This is another very important design. This fused membrane is called a *mesentery*. Mesenteries help secure organs to the body wall and hold them in the proper position so that they won't twist while also suspending them to allow them room to expand and to slide along other organs. These mesenteries are also a pathway by which nerves and blood vessels reach the organs suspended by them.

Regulation of the Digestive System

Your digestive system is sometimes very, very busy, and other times it is almost resting. How does it know when to get busy, or what it should do when presented with a chewed-up hamburger? You have probably been told that you should not swim right after you eat a big

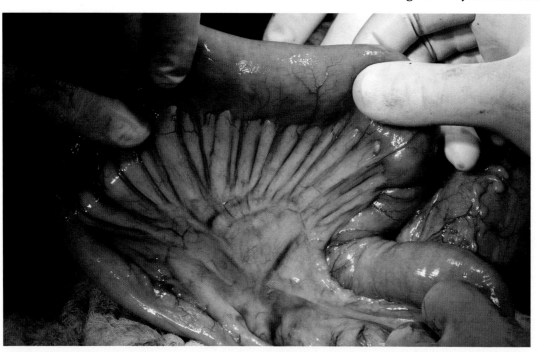

Small intestine with mesentery

meal. That is because your digestive system will be very busy and, if you suddenly divert most of the blood and oxygen it needs to do its work to your arms and legs for a vigorous swim, you might get a painful cramp as your GI tract protests the interruption.

Peritonitis

Peritonitis is a condition resulting from an acute inflammation of the peritoneum. This is a serious medical condition and is most often (although not always) the result of bacterial contamination of the abdominal cavity. The contamination can be the result of leakage from a burst ulcer or from a ruptured diverticulum in the colon. One of the most common causes of peritonitis is bacterial leakage from a ruptured appendix.

Symptoms of peritonitis include abdominal pain and fever. Patients with peritonitis often exhibit significant pain during examination of the abdomen. Any movement of the abdominal wall is very painful to someone with an inflamed peritoneum.

Peritonitis can also result from penetrating injuries to the abdominal wall. Violent trauma to the abdomen, such as stabbing or gunshots, are always dangerous, but the risk of dying from them was even worse in the past. Even if trauma victims did not bleed to death right away, contamination of the peritoneal cavity by bacteria would soon cause peritonitis. Modern surgical procedures and the discovery of antibiotics have dramatically decreased the mortality rate from peritonitis, whether due to disease or trauma.

Treatment of peritonitis includes intravenous fluids and intensive antibiotic therapy, often with multiple antibiotics. Sometimes surgical intervention is required, even in those cases unrelated to trauma. Surgery may be needed to correct the cause of the problem (i.e., fix the leak) or to drain pus from a localized abscess. Peritonitis today is usually treatable. However, in severe cases, it can still be fatal.

So before moving into a detailed exploration of the digestive system, we need to understand the basics of how this system is controlled, or regulated.

Some of the activity of the digestive system is under local control. That is to say that some mechanisms that control digestion can be found in the digestive system itself. The lining of the GI tract contains lots of special receptors. Some are triggered by stretching of the surrounding structures, like when a rounded ball of chewed food — called a *bolus* — enters the lumen. Other receptors are triggered by the presence of certain hormones or certain types of food. Greasy food, for instance, requires certain chemicals to process it, chemicals not needed to process saltine crackers. Food leaving the stomach has been mixed with a strong acid, and changes in the acid levels in the contents of the lumen can also be detected by receptors in the GI tract walls.

When triggered, some receptors stimulate smooth muscle to contract. Others cause glands to increase or decrease release of digestive enzymes or other chemicals. Some receptors, when stimulated, trigger release of certain hormones into the blood. You see, lots of things happen in the walls of the organs in the digestive system.

Further, the GI tract has its own nervous system, called the *enteric nervous system*. These neurons found in the walls of the GI tract are essential to adequate regulation of the digestive system. It has been estimated that the enteric nervous system contains 100 million neurons (No, I don't know who counted them . . .)! Some have gone as far as to call this collection of neurons the "gut brain." These neurons help control not only the motility of the GI tract, but also the secretory activity of cells in the epithelium.

Lastly, there are control mechanisms involving the central nervous system. These bring a level of control from outside the digestive tract. It is

3

ANATOMY OF THE DIGESTIVE SYSTEM

As with any good journey, the best place to start is at the beginning. We will therefore follow the path that food takes as we explore the anatomy and function of each part of the GI tract. Along the way, we will take a few detours to explore nearby accessory digestive organs.

Here we go . . .

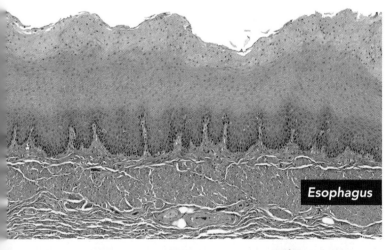
Esophagus

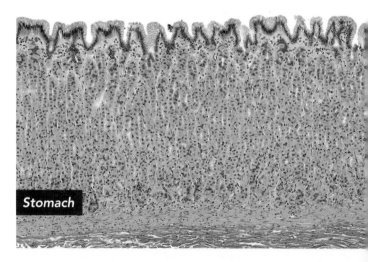
Stomach

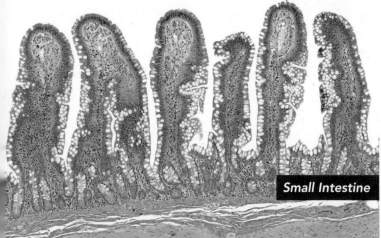
Small Intestine

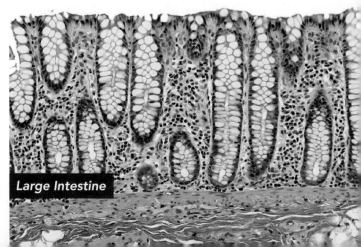
Large Intestine

The Mouth

The obvious starting point of the digestive system is the mouth. After all, if there were not a place for food to enter the digestive system, then what would be the point?

The mouth has a vital role to play in many functions of the body. It is vital to speaking (and singing, of course). The mouth also has a role in breathing. For our purposes here, we will limit our discussion to the roles the mouth plays in digestion.

The mouth, also called the oral cavity, is bounded by the lips anteriorly (in front), the cheeks laterally (on each side), the palate superiorly (on top), and the tongue inferiorly (on the bottom).

The lips form the opening to the oral cavity. This opening is formed by a circular skeletal muscle called the *orbicularis oris*. The lips are covered by skin on the outside but by mucous membrane on the inside of the mouth. It is best if the lips are closed while you chew and swallow to prevent food from escaping. As might be expected, the lips, containing skeletal muscle, are under voluntary control.

The cheeks form the lateral walls of the oral cavity. In each cheek is found connective tissue and the *buccinator* muscle. The cheeks aid in digestion by pushing food to the proper position to make chewing as efficient as possible.

The superior (upper) boundary of the mouth is formed by the hard and soft palates. This is called the "roof" of the mouth. The hard palate forms the front part of this roof. The hard palate is a bony structure covered by a mucous membrane. The hard palate separates the oral cavity from the nasal cavity. Behind the hard palate is the soft palate. It

TAKING A CLOSER LOOK
The Mouth

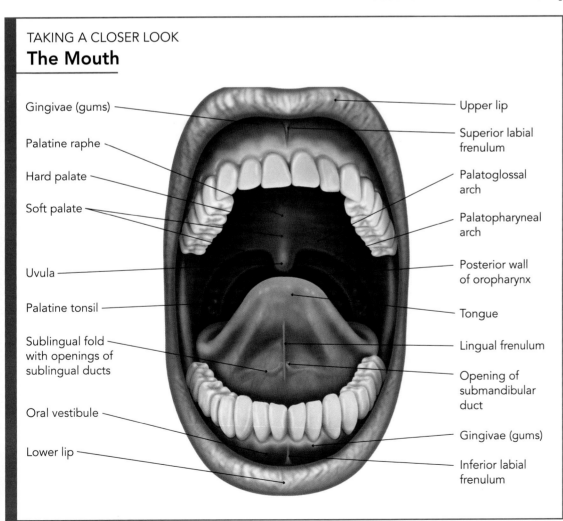

- Gingivae (gums)
- Palatine raphe
- Hard palate
- Soft palate
- Uvula
- Palatine tonsil
- Sublingual fold with openings of sublingual ducts
- Oral vestibule
- Lower lip

- Upper lip
- Superior labial frenulum
- Palatoglossal arch
- Palatopharyneal arch
- Posterior wall of oropharynx
- Tongue
- Lingual frenulum
- Opening of submandibular duct
- Gingivae (gums)
- Inferior labial frenulum

is made up of skeletal muscle covered by mucous membrane. The soft palate moves during swallowing to seal off the nasal passage while food moves from the mouth into the esophagus. Without your soft palate, every time you swallowed something, part of it would squirt up behind your nose.

The Tongue

The floor of the mouth is formed by the tongue. It is one of the three accessory digestive organs found in the mouth.

The tongue is composed of two sets of skeletal muscles. That tells you right away that the tongue is under your control.

The first set, the intrinsic muscles, are contained within the tongue itself. These muscles allow the shape of the tongue to be altered as conditions warrant. The intrinsic muscles can cause the tongue to lengthen or shorten, to become thicker or thinner.

The other set of muscles are extrinsic muscles. These muscles are attached to bone at one end and to the tongue on the other. Contraction of the extrinsic muscles helps change the position of the tongue within the mouth. When you stick out your tongue and pull it back in, you are utilizing these extrinsic muscles. If you wag your tongue from side to side, again these extrinsic muscles are responsible.

What bone do you think the tongue's extrinsic muscles are attached to? They are attached to the hyoid bone, a small U-shaped bone below the floor of the mouth. Many muscles hold the hyoid bone in place. The tongue's extrinsic muscles as well as muscles in the floor of the mouth, throat muscles, and the voice box (larynx) are anchored to it.

The tongue is rather rough looking when you examine it. There are many little bumps on the surface. These bumps are called *papillae*, and there are several types. *Filiform* (or thread-like) papillae cover the front two-thirds of the tongue. Mushroom

TAKING A CLOSER LOOK
Tongue Muscles

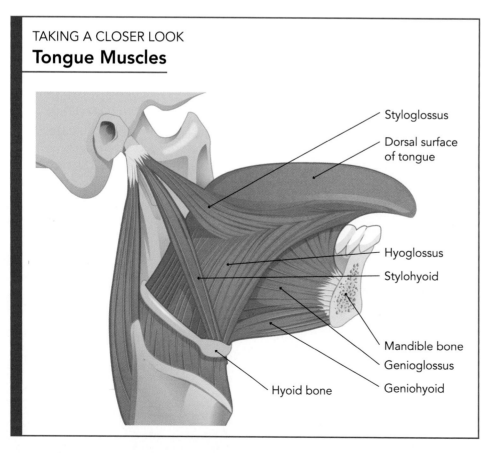

- Styloglossus
- Dorsal surface of tongue
- Hyoglossus
- Stylohyoid
- Mandible bone
- Genioglossus
- Geniohyoid
- Hyoid bone

shaped papillae known as *fungiform* ("fungi" meaning mushroom-like) papillae are diffusely scattered across the surface of the tongue. The *foliate* papillae have a small ridge-like appearance along the sides of the tongue near the rear. Finally, there are *circumvallate* papillae. These are more nodular in shape and are found in a V-shaped row across the rear of the tongue.

Taste buds are found in fungiform, foliate, and circumvallate papillae. Filiform papillae have no taste buds.

The tongue and cheeks help position food in the mouth during chewing. Also, tongue movement helps push food back in the mouth to be swallowed.

The Teeth

The teeth are perhaps the most easily recognized accessory digestive organs. After all, teeth are visible when we smile or speak or say "cheese!" when having our picture taken.

TAKING A CLOSER LOOK
The Tongue

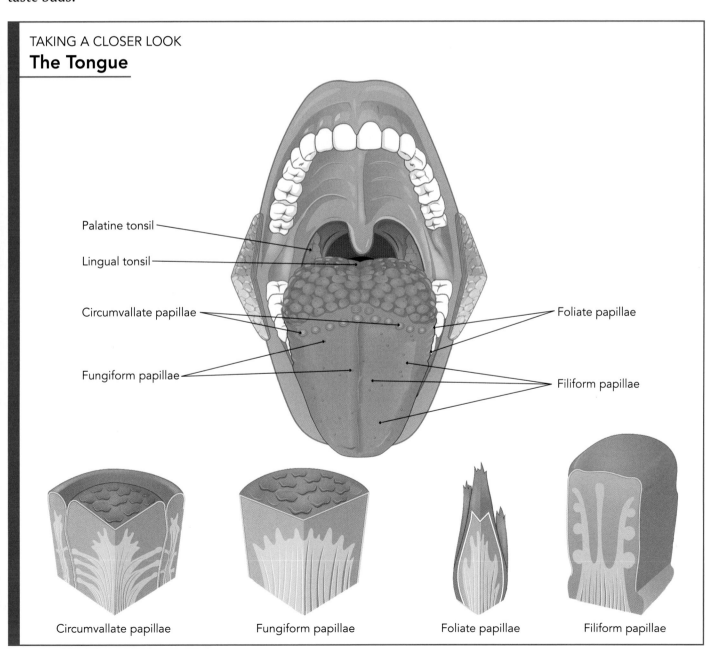

Palatine tonsil

Lingual tonsil

Circumvallate papillae

Fungiform papillae

Foliate papillae

Filiform papillae

Circumvallate papillae   Fungiform papillae   Foliate papillae   Filiform papillae

The function of teeth in the process of digestion is also quite obvious. As we chew, the teeth break down larger pieces of food into smaller and smaller pieces. These smaller bits of food have more total surface area than larger ones. Digestive chemicals and enzymes act on this expanded surface area to more efficiently digest well-chewed food. Perhaps you have been told to chew your food 40 times before swallowing. This may be a bit of overkill, but, nonetheless, the more thoroughly food is chewed, the better for your digestion.

Each tooth has three major regions: the crown, the neck, and the root. The *crown* is the part of the tooth that is visible. That is, the crown is the portion of the tooth outside the gums. The *root* is the part of the tooth that is anchored inside the bony socket in either the mandible (for the lower teeth) or the maxilla (for the upper teeth). The tooth's *neck* is simply the part of the tooth connecting the crown and the root. There is connective tissue and mucous membrane around the neck of the tooth that extends over the bone in which the tooth is anchored. This mucous membrane-covered connective tissue is called the *gingiva*, or *gums*.

The crown of a tooth is covered with *enamel*. Enamel is the hardest substance in the body, and it is very durable. This durability allows the tooth to withstand the wear and tear of chewing (hopefully for a lifetime). Enamel consists mostly of a crystalline form of calcium phosphate called hydroxyapatite, along with a small amount of protein. The protein found in tooth enamel differs from the collagen protein found in bone. Enamel is produced while the tooth is forming, before it emerges, and it cannot be replaced. (Trying to rebuild lost enamel is an area of dental research.)

Underneath the crown's enamel is a substance called *dentin*. Dentin makes up the majority of the volume of a tooth. It is made of connective tissue that is highly mineralized, and it is a lot like bone. Below the gum line, the dentin is protected by another hard substance called *cementum*. Specialized cells continually make more cementum to replace it as it wears out, which is a good thing since the fibers that hold your teeth in must attach to the tooth's cementum.

TAKING A CLOSER LOOK
Tooth Anatomy

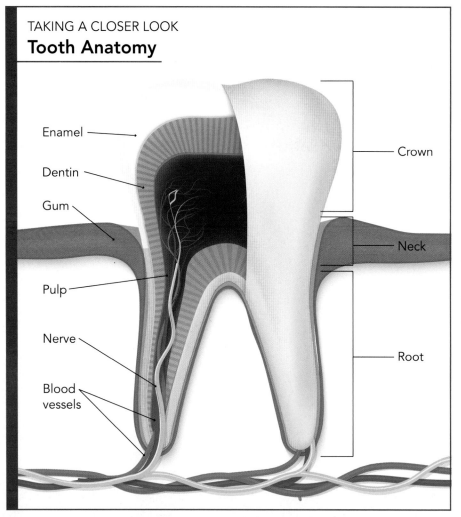

Enamel

Dentin

Gum

Pulp

Nerve

Blood vessels

Crown

Neck

Root

Within the dentin is the pulp cavity. In the pulp cavity is found nerves and blood vessels. The nerves obviously provide pain sensation. Biting down on something very hard or very cold may give you a painful warning to take more care with your teeth. And an infected tooth hurts a lot. The blood vessels in the pulp provide nutrition for the tooth. At the bottom of each root is a small opening through which the nerves and blood vessels enter the tooth.

So, what keeps your healthy teeth from simply falling out every time you bite down on something? Each tooth is secured in its socket by a complex and highly organized collection of connective tissue fibers known as the *periodontal ligament*. These fibers connect the cementum covering the root to the bony socket's connective tissue lining. In addition to being connected to bone by the periodontal ligament's fibers, the cementum is also attached to the gingiva, or gums, by gingival fibers. Anything that weakens the tissues in these connections — such as loss of minerals in the cementum or chronic gum inflammation — increases the risk of losing teeth in later life.

Both enamel and cementum contain fluoride, which is incorporated into their calcium-containing structures. Fluoride makes these substances even more durable, and facilitates the deposition of calcium and phosphate ions back into the enamel and cementum if some of these minerals are lost. Cementum contains a higher percentage of fluoride than any other mineralized tissue in the body. Fluoride is present in varying amounts in ordinary rainwater, in tea leaves, and in some foods, such as raisins and potatoes. Many communities add fluoride to drinking water to decrease the incidence of tooth decay, though this is controversial in some places.

If you allow your enamel to become demineralized, you may develop cavities — holes in your tooth enamel. It is possible to damage the enamel beyond repair through poor dental hygiene or even by chewing on materials so hard that they damage and wear away the enamel. Unprotected by enamel, tooth decay can become severe. You may even develop an infection in decayed teeth, eventually losing them completely. The acids produced by bacteria while they digest the sugars in your food eat away at the minerals that make enamel hard. If you fail to frequently floss and brush away food residue, sugary substances, and tartar-forming bacteria, the acids produced by the bacteria can eat away at the enamel as surely as an egg soaking in vinegar loses its hard shell.

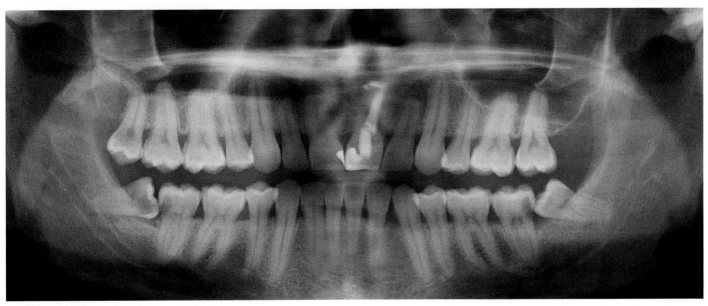

Full mouth x-ray

Remember, enamel is formed on the tooth's crown before it emerges from beneath the gum, so you might think that demineralization of your enamel is irreversible. Indeed, enamel cannot be replaced, but some of the minerals in it can be put back. God designed your tooth enamel to remineralize itself by incorporating minerals — calcium, phosphate, and fluoride ions—dissolved in your saliva. Because enamel is not connected to your bloodstream, only the minerals dissolved in your saliva participate in this remineralization process. Taking mineral supplements in the form of pills does not help your tooth enamel.

The demineralization and remineralization of tooth enamel is an ongoing dynamic process. Remineralization is helped along by good dental hygiene, which keeps your teeth from prolonged exposure to acids. The acids produced by bacteria not only dissolve the minerals in your tooth enamel but also make it hard for teeth to recapture the lost minerals.

Saliva, which is produced by several glands, neutralizes acids. This is important because remineralization cannot happen in an acidic environment. It is important to keep your teeth and gums as clean as possible by brushing and flossing away bacteria-containing plaque, food particles, and sugary residue that feed bacteria as soon as possible after eating or drinking anything containing sugar.

Nobody wants their teeth to rot. After all, how can you chew your food if your teeth fall out? And the pain of infected and decaying teeth can be pretty bad. Nowadays, we know we should brush and floss. Before modern times, many ancient people also knew they needed to clean their teeth and figured out ways

Toothbrushes primitive and modern

Tooth Decay

Have you ever had a cavity? You are fortunate if you haven't. Unfortunately, this is a very common problem.

Tooth decay, also known as *dental caries*, is the result of the breaking down of the hard tissues of the tooth, primarily the enamel and the dentin. This process begins as plaque starts to build up on the surface of a tooth. *Plaque* is made up of bits of food and other debris, and bacteria love to live in it. The bacteria in the mouth begin to break down the debris in the plaque, mainly sugars. The bacteria produce acids that ultimately cause the breakdown of enamel and dentin. This loss of tissue leads to cavities.

Dental plaque can cause further problems when it occurs near the gums. As the plaque builds up, it can cause inflammation of the gums. This is called gingivitis.

Major risk factors for tooth decay include a diet high in sugar and poor dental hygiene.

Fortunately, dental caries can be prevented to a large degree. Obviously, decreasing the amount of sweets in the diet would be an important step. This doesn't mean don't eat sweets at all (what fun would that be?). It means eat sweets only now and then.

Equally important for prevention of tooth decay is proper brushing and flossing. Brushing of the teeth regularly, after every meal, is very, very important. This helps clear

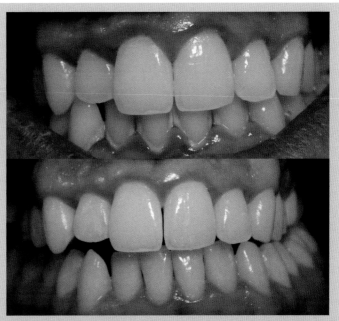

away the bacteria and debris that build up on the surface of the teeth. Also, daily flossing of the teeth helps remove the plaque that builds up between the teeth.

Proper care of your teeth cannot be stressed enough. It needs to be remembered that while the enamel of a tooth can be somewhat remineralized if you exercise good oral hygiene, it cannot be replaced. The cells that produce enamel deteriorate shortly before a tooth erupts. So once enamel is damaged, the body has no mechanism for replacement. Once significant decay has occurred, consultation with a dentist is required. If you have ever had a cavity filled, you know about this. Filling a cavity patches the problem to protect the underlying tissues, but it cannot put back the enamel that is lost.

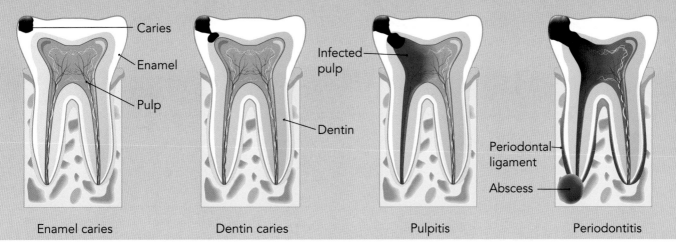

Enamel caries   Dentin caries   Pulpitis   Periodontitis

Caries — Enamel — Pulp — Infected pulp — Dentin — Periodontal ligament — Abscess

to do it. Ancient Egyptians and Babylonians — like the ones talked about in the Bible — cleaned their teeth by chewing on the frayed ends of twigs. Some Egyptians were even buried with their toothsticks, lest they enter the afterlife with poor dental hygiene. During the Middle Ages, the Chinese developed actual tooth*brushes* made of the bristles from pigs' necks, and pig bristles were commonly used to make toothbrushes in Europe until modern synthetic materials were developed. Toothpaste is also an ancient invention. The ancient Egyptians developed the oldest known recipe for toothpaste. It contained dried iris flower, mint, salt, and pepper. Examination

of ancient Egyptian remains shows that Egyptians didn't have much of a problem with tooth cavities.

Other things can also damage enamel. In ancient Egypt, for instance, though tooth decay was not all that common, erosion of tooth enamel was a big problem. Worn away enamel left the underlying dentin unprotected, leading to rampant tooth abscesses. *Abscesses* are areas of trapped infection, often containing pus. They hurt. Archaeologists have found that Egyptian flour, used to bake bread, contained a lot of stony grit, possibly from the soft sandstone used to grind grain or from regular contamination by blowing sand. Years of chewing

Healthy Gums? Healthy Heart?

It is certainly reasonable that we should take steps to care for our teeth. After all, going to the dentist to get cavities filled, damaged teeth crowned, or infected teeth rescued with root canals is not fun. And once a permanent tooth is lost, it is lost forever. People have known for thousands of years that the bad breath associated with poor oral hygiene is just plain unpleasant. Ancient Romans used to include odor-absorbing charcoal in their toothpaste. However, there may be another very important health issue to be considered here. There is some evidence that poor oral hygiene can lead to heart disease.

People who develop vascular problems — that is, problems relating to blood vessels, especially arteries — very often have poor blood flow to the heart and/or brain. This often leads to a heart attack or a stroke. Over the years, research has shown that one of the primary causes of damage to the lining of these blood vessels is chronic inflammation. The damage to the endothelial lining of the blood vessel can lead to a blockage. This blockage lowers the flow of blood through the artery.

So how does this relate to gum disease? Well, a common kind of chronic inflammation is gum disease, or gingivitis. The substances responsible for the inflammation in the gums can be released into the bloodstream and possibly promote inflammation in other parts of the body. Some doctors believe that these chemicals may be a risk factor for heart disease and stroke.

Although there are strong reasons to suggest a relationship between the two, at present, there is no definite research showing a link between gum disease and heart disease. This will be an ongoing issue for researchers as time goes on.

For now, this is just another reason that you should take care of your teeth and gums. Develop good oral hygiene habits now. As you get older you will be glad you did.

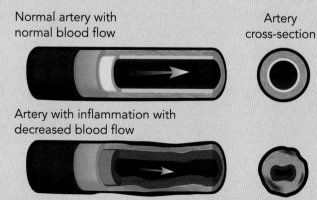

Normal artery with normal blood flow

Artery cross-section

Artery with inflammation with decreased blood flow

food like this took its toll on Egyptian teeth, and no amount of brushing with good toothpaste could put back the enamel ground away daily by gritty food. People in many other ancient cultures also developed toothpaste. Unfortunately, some of their toothpastes contained ground pumice stone. The Greeks and Romans were particularly eager to scrub their teeth with material like this. Such abrasive toothpastes did a nice job of whitening their teeth, sanding away stains, but it ground away at the enamel, doubtless leading to eventual tooth loss.

Everybody has two sets of teeth in their lifetime. Actually, some people end up with *more* than two sets if you count dentures. So, let's say everybody has two sets of *naturally occurring* teeth in their lifetime.

Our first teeth are called primary teeth. They are also called baby teeth or milk teeth. These teeth are already present in a baby's jaw at birth, hidden deep beneath the gums. These teeth begin to erupt (this means to appear or become visible) at about 6

months of age, and all 20 primary teeth are usually present by three years of age. These consist of 8 incisors, 4 so-called canine teeth, and 8 molars. Incisor teeth are shaped for cutting through food, molars for grinding food, and canines for both.

As permanent teeth develop, the roots of the primary teeth that will be lost to make room for them dissolve away, allowing the baby teeth to loosen. Most often, the primary teeth have fallen out by age 12. It is very important to take good care of the primary teeth even though they will eventually fall out. Children need them to chew properly. Cavities can lead to painful infections and tooth loss. And God designed the primary teeth as the place-holders for the more numerous permanent teeth. Their presence helps the permanent teeth remain aligned properly as they erupt. Loss of baby teeth too early can cause the permanent teeth lurking beneath the gums to shift and eventually come in very crooked, crooked enough to make chewing inefficient.

TAKING A CLOSER LOOK
Dentition — The Arrangement of the Teeth

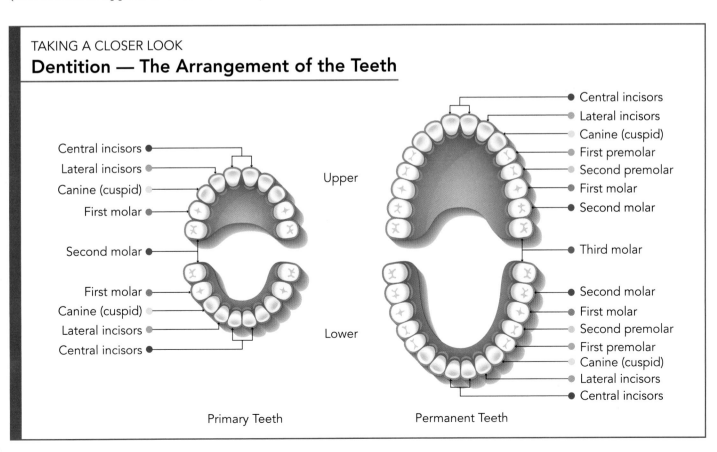

Central incisors
Lateral incisors
Canine (cuspid)
First molar
Second molar
First molar
Canine (cuspid)
Lateral incisors
Central incisors

Upper

Lower

Central incisors
Lateral incisors
Canine (cuspid)
First premolar
Second premolar
First molar
Second molar
Third molar
Second molar
First molar
Second premolar
First premolar
Canine (cuspid)
Lateral incisors
Central incisors

Primary Teeth

Permanent Teeth

Permanent teeth begin to erupt around ages 7 or 8. There are 32 permanent teeth, and the buds of these teeth are present long before birth. The permanent teeth are generally all present by age 21. Adults ordinarily grow 8 incisors, 4 canine teeth, 8 bicuspids, and 12 molars. The third molars, also called wisdom teeth, on occasion do not erupt. We call the permanent teeth "permanent" because God designed them to be permanent. You are meant to keep them for a lifetime. But you must take proper care of them if they are to last.

Salivary Glands

The salivary glands are a type of gland known as an exocrine gland. A *gland* is an organ that produces a useful chemical substance. An endocrine gland secretes its products directly into the blood stream to be carried throughout the body, but an *exocrine gland* secretes its product by means of a *duct* — a small tube — directly into the place where it's needed. The *salivary glands* do precisely that. They produce saliva and deliver it into the oral cavity by means of small ducts.

Although there are several minor salivary glands, the three primary sets are the parotid glands, the submandibular glands, and the sublingual glands.

The largest of the salivary glands are the *parotid glands*. There is one parotid gland on each side of the face. It is located under the skin just anterior to — in front of — the ear. Each secretes saliva into the oral cavity though the parotid duct. These glands are responsible for about 20 percent of the total amount of saliva produced. The parotid gland is particularly important for reasons other than saliva production. Branches of the facial nerve run through the parotid

TAKING A CLOSER LOOK
Salivary Glands

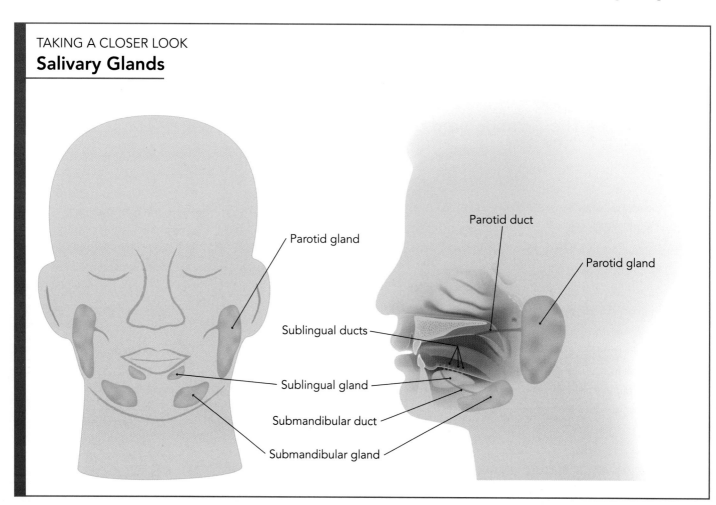

Parotid gland

Parotid duct

Parotid gland

Sublingual ducts

Sublingual gland

Submandibular duct

Submandibular gland

Parotitis

Parotitis is the inflammation of one or both of the parotid glands. It is characterized by pain and swelling of the gland. There is tenderness to *palpation* (touching) of the cheek overlying the gland. Quite often there is fever, fatigue, and pain with chewing.

The most common cause of parotitis is a particular viral infection called mumps. There is no current treatment for mumps, and it usually lasts about a week. One of the vaccines commonly administered to children is given to prevent mumps.

Parotitis due to bacterial infection can also occur. Pain, fever, and swelling are also seen with bacterial parotitis. However, treatment with antibiotics is very important in these cases.

In elderly patients, extreme dehydration has been shown to contribute to a non-infectious type of parotitis. Other causes of parotitis include autoimmune disease (such as Sjogren's syndrome), tuberculosis, blockage of the parotid duct, or even malignancy.

Healthy child   Child with mumps

gland, so surgery on the parotid, say to remove a tumor, can result in paralysis of the face on that side.

The *submandibular glands* are located under the mandible — the lower jaw — near the rear. Not surprisingly, the submandibular glands empty into the mouth via the submandibular ducts. About 70 percent of saliva is produced by these glands.

Finally, we have the *sublingual glands*. As the name suggests — *sub* meaning "under" and *lingua* meaning "tongue" — they are found below the tongue. Rather than having a primary duct, the sublingual glands empty into the floor of the mouth via 10–12 smaller ducts.

Saliva

Saliva is a watery substance produced by the salivary glands. Everyone knows what saliva is, but not

everyone is aware of how important it is to the digestive process.

Saliva helps moisten the inside of the oral cavity. In fact, saliva is composed of 99 percent water. In addition, it contains important enzymes, antimicrobials, and ions. The enzymes start the digestive process for some of the foods we eat. The antimicrobials in saliva include several immunoglobulins (antibodies) that discourage bacteria from sticking to things as well as proteins that destroy bacterial cell membranes. The ions include dissolved minerals that are used to restore the minerals in tooth enamel as well as ions that *buffer*, or neutralize, the acids produced by bacteria that live in our mouths.

Saliva helps protect the mucous membrane lining the mouth and also prevents food from sticking to the surface of the cheeks and tongue. Further, the saliva moistens food. This helps keep the food in a small lump (often called a "bolus"), making chewing and swallowing more efficient. Saliva helps you taste your food by dissolving substances in food. These dissolved substances can then be detected by the taste buds.

Cleansing of the mouth is aided by saliva. It helps wash away waste products and debris. When sticky *plaque* — a mass of bacteria and their products — adheres to a tooth, the acids produced by bacteria multiplying in it build up underneath. If not removed, plaque calcifies and hardens into *tartar*. Since the saliva cannot get under plaque to neutralize and wash away the acids, the acids eat

away at the minerals in the tooth enamel, and tooth decay can result.

Beyond making chewing more efficient, saliva also helps begin the actual process of breaking down food. Saliva contains the enzyme amylase. Amylase helps break down starch into the sugars it is made of. Starches are not completely digested in the mouth, but the process starts there.

Another sort of enzyme — a fat-digesting lipase — is produced by tiny glands beneath some of the papillae on the tongue. This *lingual lipase* begins the first step of fat digestion.

Saliva and Amylase

There is a very simple way to show that there is at least some digestion that takes place in the mouth itself. Even before swallowing.

Here's what to do. Get a piece of white bread or a saltine cracker and take a big bite. Then begin to chew this in your mouth. Don't swallow it. Just keep slowly chewing. Pay close attention and see if you don't begin to sense a sweet taste in your mouth. This sweet taste is the result of the enzyme amylase.

Amylase is found in saliva. It causes the breakdown of starch in our food into sugars. So, what began in your mouth as either bland or slightly salty, became sweet.

All because of amylase.

How is Salivation Controlled?

The production of saliva has been estimated to be between one and one and a half liters per day. The rate of production of saliva varies throughout the day. This seems quite logical. We need more saliva when we eat and less at other times.

So how is saliva production regulated?

Regulation of saliva production is primarily under the control of the parasympathetic nervous system. The presence of food in the mouth triggers chemical receptors. These receptors send signals to the brain stem, and the incoming signals are processed. Motor impulses are then sent to the salivary glands by way of fibers in the facial and glossopharyngeal nerves. This motor input stimulates the salivary glands to produce more saliva.

Another type of receptor in the mouth is a mechanoreceptor. Movement triggers a mechanoreceptor. As food is chewed, movement of the tongue, cheeks, and jaw muscles stimulates mechanoreceptors. Subsequently, signals are sent to the brain stem that, like chemoreceptors, ultimately stimulate saliva production.

advertising a big juicy hamburger. For your author, just thinking about French vanilla ice cream is all it takes. Thus, higher level functions in the brain (learning, memory, experience, etc.) also play a role in saliva production.

Well, if saliva production can be stimulated, can it also be inhibited? Yes, it can. Inhibition of the salivary glands can occur by means of the sympathetic nervous system. This decrease in saliva often happens as part of what is known as the "fight or flight" response. Hopefully, you will remember this from Volume Three of *Wonders of the Human Body*. When under stress, certain less-needed systems are inhibited. If you have ever had a really dry mouth before a big test or before you were to sing a solo at church, you have felt this "fight or flight" response in action.

Interestingly, saliva production can often be stimulated by the mere sight or smell (or even thought) of food. Have you ever noticed how your mouth begins to water when you smell something delicious cooking on the barbecue grill? Perhaps the same thing happened when you saw a billboard

Xerostomia

If you ever need confirmation of the important role saliva plays in our daily health, you need only meet someone who suffers from *xerostomia*. This is also known as "dry mouth syndrome." In many cases, it is the direct result of an abnormally low production of saliva.

A low output of saliva can be the unfortunate result of aging. As people get older, things don't work as well as they once did. Salivary glands may decrease their output with age. Side effects of some medications also often include dry mouth. Further, some connective tissue diseases, such as Sjogren's syndrome or systemic lupus erythematosus, can cause xerostomia.

Xerostomia is often debilitating. Remember, saliva neutralizes bacteria-produced acids and helps remineralize tooth enamel. Without adequate saliva production, sufferers of xerostomia have a much higher rate of tooth decay and tissue breakdown in the mouth. They are also more vulnerable to oral fungal infections. They may have a constant soreness and tingling sensation in the mouth. Loss of taste sensation, difficulty chewing, difficulty swallowing, and chronic bad breath (*halitosis*) are associated with inadequate saliva production.

Treatment of xerostomia can be challenging. Treatment of underlying conditions is an obvious first step, but of course there is no cure for being elderly. Changing long-term medications to minimize side effects is another common intervention. Saliva substitutes help some patients. In addition, some treatments are designed to directly stimulate saliva production.

Have you noticed that everyone — your dentist, your parents, even toothpaste commercials — encourages you to brush your teeth *as soon as possible* after eating or drinking something sugary? There is a good reason for this. Once you have finished eating, saliva production decreases dramatically. At the same time, the bacteria living in your mouth begin pumping out lots of acid as they feed on the sugar residue in your mouth. Saliva production doesn't return to normal levels for about 20 to 30 minutes, giving time for these acids to begin demineralizing and damaging the protective coverings on your teeth. If you brush, however, you stop this destructive process.

Mastication is just a fancy way of saying chewing. This is where mechanical digestion begins.

Food is taken into the mouth, and the lips are closed. Next, as the jaw opens and closes, the teeth tear and grind the food. The closing of the jaw is primarily due to the actions of the powerful *masseter* muscle, with some assistance from the *temporalis* muscle. Side to side movements of the jaw, which help grind food, are due to the *medial pterygoid* muscle and the *lateral pterygoid* muscle.

As mastication continues, larger pieces of food become smaller and smaller in preparation for swallowing. Movement of the cheeks and tongue constantly position and reposition food to keep it between the teeth. At the same time, saliva is constantly mixed with this bolus of food. Salivary amylase and lipase begin digesting any starches and fats in the food.

TAKING A CLOSER LOOK
Muscles of Mastication

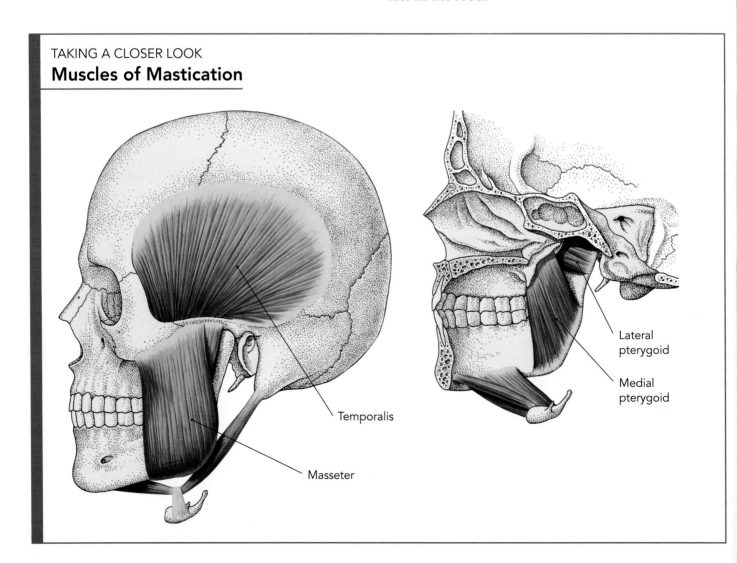

Temporalis

Masseter

Lateral pterygoid

Medial pterygoid

TAKING A CLOSER LOOK
The Pharynx

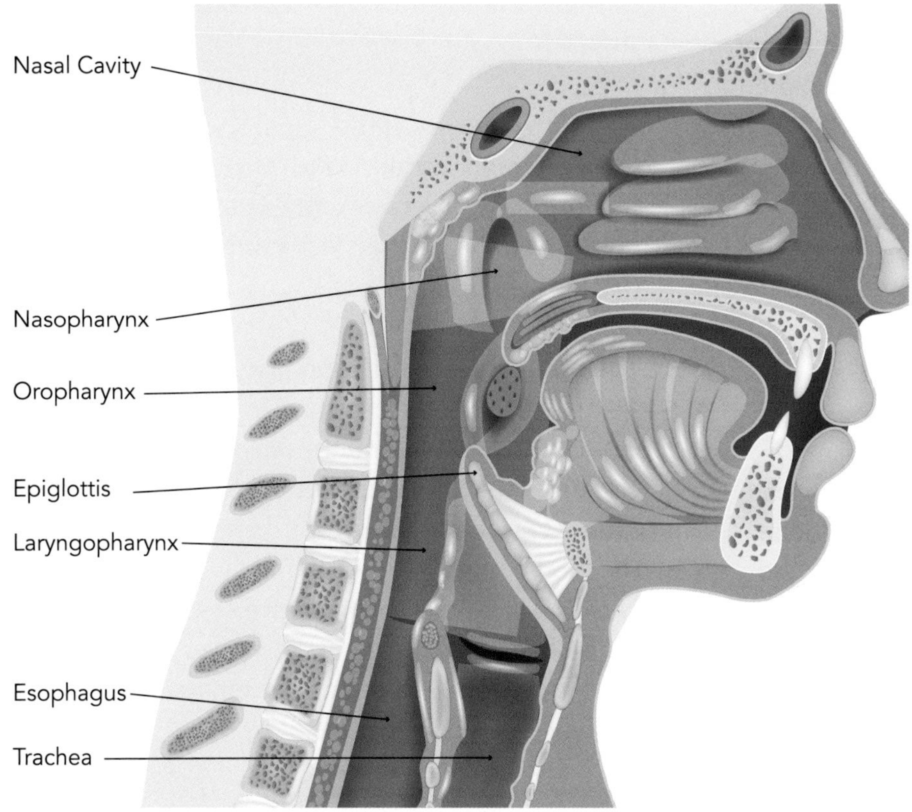

Nasal Cavity

Nasopharynx

Oropharynx

Epiglottis

Laryngopharynx

Esophagus

Trachea

TAKING A CLOSER LOOK
The Esophagus in the Diaphragm

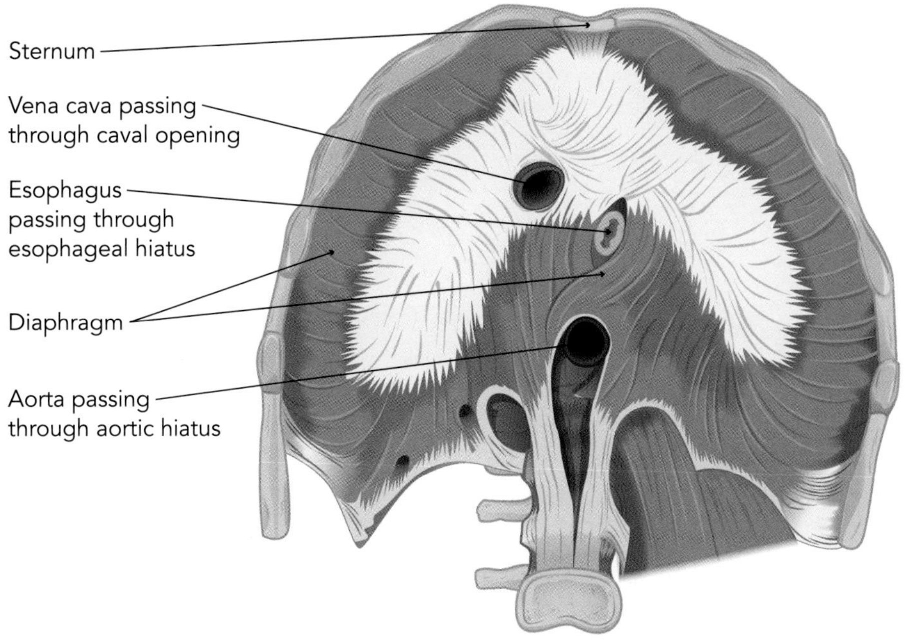

Sternum

Vena cava passing through caval opening

Esophagus passing through esophageal hiatus

Diaphragm

Aorta passing through aortic hiatus

When sufficiently chewed, the bolus of food is pushed to the rear of the mouth in preparation for swallowing.

The Pharynx

The posterior portion of the oral cavity empties into the pharynx. This area is often called the "throat." The *pharynx* is a funnel-shaped tube that extends down to the level of the larynx ("voice box") and the esophagus, the tube that carries food and drink to your stomach. The walls of the pharynx are made of skeletal muscle and, like most surfaces inside your mouth and nose, are covered by mucous membrane.

The pharynx is composed of three regions: the nasopharynx, the oropharynx, and the laryngopharynx.

The *nasopharynx* is the superior portion of the larynx and extends from the rear of the nasal cavity and ends at the level of the soft palate. The nasopharynx is not part of the digestive system and plays no role in the processing of food. However, on rare occasions it does become a factor when swallowing. Remember, the soft palate — the soft flap of tissue behind the hard palate — moves to seal off your nasopharynx as you swallow. Have you ever started laughing or coughing at the exact moment you were trying to swallow something? In these instances, the soft palate often does not seal off the nasal cavity well enough to prevent the food from finding its way into your nose.

The *oropharynx* is the portion from the soft palate down to the level of the hyoid bone. The hyoid bone is located deep beneath the tongue at about the level of the chin.

The *laryngopharynx* begins where the oropharynx ends, at the level of the hyoid bone. It extends down to the opening of the esophagus.

The Esophagus

The esophagus is a muscular tube that connects the pharynx to the stomach. It is about 10 inches long. The upper part of the esophagus is located behind the trachea, which carries air to your lungs. It continues down through your chest behind (posterior to) the lungs and heart and in front of (anterior to) the vertebral column. To reach the abdominal cavity, the esophagus must pass through an opening in the diaphragm known as the *esophageal hiatus*. The word "hiatus" refers to a gap or an interruption. The large sheet-like muscle of the diaphragm must have this opening to allow the esophagus to reach the stomach.

Beginning here with the top of the esophagus, we see the alimentary canal — or GI tract — walls contain the four basic layers described earlier. Remember, the oral cavity and pharynx have different microscopic tissue layers in their walls.

The inner layer of the esophagus is the *mucosa*. Remember, the mucosa consists of the *epithelium*, the *lamina propria,* and the *muscularis mucosae*. The epithelial layer surrounds the lumen of the esophagus and is the layer in direct contact with the food being swallowed. Unlike the later portions of the GI tract, no nutrients are absorbed through the walls of the esophagus. However, the epithelial layer protects the esophagus from being damaged by swallowed food as it whizzes by.

TAKING A CLOSER LOOK
The Esophagus Cross-section

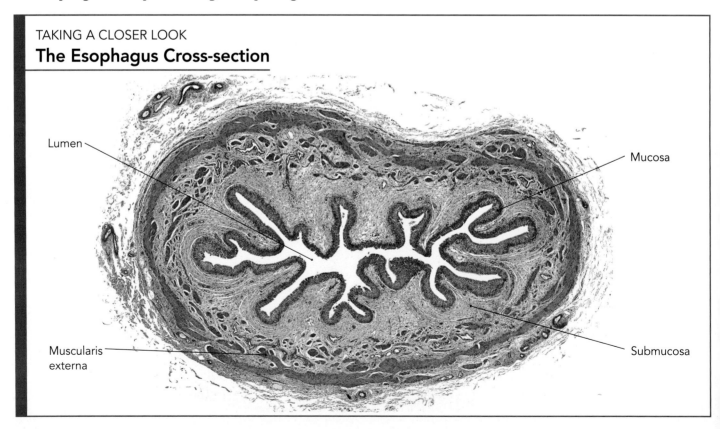

Lumen

Mucosa

Muscularis externa

Submucosa

Moving outward in the esophageal wall we come to the *submucosa*. Connective tissue and blood vessels are located in the submucosa along with glands that secrete mucous. This mucous lubricates the esophagus to aid in swallowing.

Next is the *muscularis externa*. In the upper third of the esophagus, this layer is made of skeletal muscle. Near the middle of the esophagus, the layer is made of both skeletal and smooth muscle. In the lower third of the esophagus, this layer is all smooth

muscle. Does this arrangement make sense to you? Recall that skeletal muscle is subject to voluntary control, and smooth muscle is not. Give that some thought, and soon we will consider why God designed the esophagus this way.

At each end of the esophagus, the muscularis is thickened to form sphincters. A *sphincter* is a ring of muscle that guards the opening at the end of a tube. These sphincters contract and relax to control the passage of food through the esophagus. The sphincter at the upper end of the esophagus is called the *upper esophageal sphincter*, and the one at the lower end, near the junction of the esophagus and the stomach, is called the *lower esophageal sphincter*. Clever, huh?

The outer layer of the esophagus is a thin layer of connective tissue called the *adventitia*. This connective tissue helps hold the esophagus in place.

Blood Supply to the Esophagus

Over its course through the thoracic cavity, the esophagus receives its arterial blood supply from several places. The upper portion of the esophagus is supplied by the *inferior thyroid artery*. The mid-portion of the esophagus is supplied with arterial blood from tiny branches from the thoracic aorta. The distal portion of the esophagus is supplied by the left *inferior phrenic artery* and the left *gastric artery*.

Venous drainage from the upper portions of the esophagus is via the *azygos* and *hemiazygos veins*. The *left gastric vein* provides venous drainage from the lower esophagus.

How Swallowing Works

We have examined the anatomy of the upper portion of the GI tract. So, let's take a moment and see how everything works together thus far.

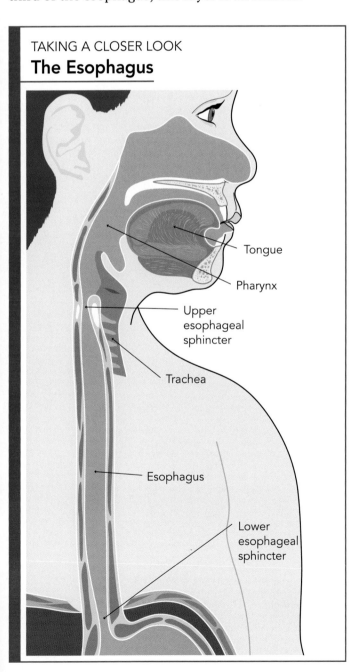

TAKING A CLOSER LOOK
The Esophagus

Tongue

Pharynx

Upper esophageal sphincter

Trachea

Esophagus

Lower esophageal sphincter

Gastroesophageal Reflux Disease

Sometimes the lower esophageal sphincter does not close completely enough to prevent the acidic contents of the stomach from flowing back into the esophagus. It may also open briefly to release air trapped in the stomach — a normal reflex response — that allows some stomach acid to escape upward into the esophagus. This back flow (known as *reflux*) can irritate the esophageal lining. This situation can result in a mild discomfort in the chest that is often referred to as *heartburn*, even though the heart is obviously not involved. More severe irritation of the esophagus from reflux can produce very severe pain that even mimics the symptoms of a heart attack.

This illness is known as gastroesophageal reflux disease, or GERD. Many thousands of visits to doctor's offices and emergency rooms each year are the result of symptoms related to GERD. Often the diagnosis can be made by taking a medical history from the patient and performing a thorough physical examination. At other times, blood tests, x-rays of the stomach and esophagus, or even examination of the lining of the esophagus and stomach with a special fiber-optic instrument (known as an *endoscope*) is needed for a precise diagnosis. *Fiber-optic* instruments allow doctors to look into tiny openings using finely drawn glass or plastic fibers to transmit light.

Risk factors for GERD include smoking, alcohol, diabetes, and obesity. In addition, some people have an anatomical abnormality in which the upper part of the stomach protrudes above the diaphragm, producing a small bulge. This bulge is known as a *hiatal hernia*. This problem can easily be seen on x-ray. It is a common cause of GERD.

GERD is most commonly treated by measures that reduce stomach acid production. This can be achieved by avoiding certain foods that stimulate stomach acid production, such as those containing chocolate or caffeine. Also, patients with GERD are advised not to lie down just after eating. This helps minimize reflux by keeping the esophagus above the level of the stomach during the most active period of digestion.

It is important that GERD be treated as effectively as possible. First of all, doctors want patients to be free of discomfort, and relief of their symptoms is a primary concern. However, left untreated, gastroesophageal reflux can lead to ulcers in the lining of the esophagus. In the most severe cases, GERD is associated with an increased risk of esophageal cancer.

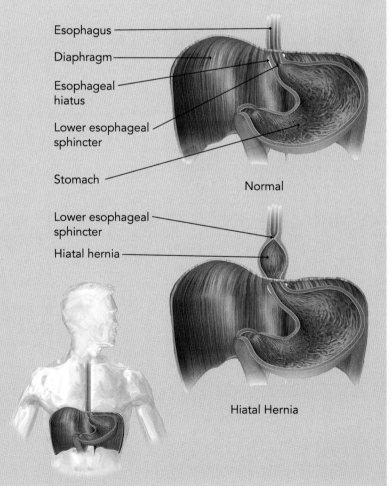

Esophagus

Diaphragm

Esophageal hiatus

Lower esophageal sphincter

Stomach

Normal

Lower esophageal sphincter

Hiatal hernia

Hiatal Hernia

To begin with, a bite of food (or a drink of water, milk, etc.) enters the mouth. The process of chewing begins. The teeth break up and grind the food into smaller and smaller bits. The tongue and cheeks play a role by keeping the bolus of food positioned properly between the teeth. Saliva helps bind the bits of ground food into a mass called a bolus. Enzymes in the saliva begin to break down the starches and some of the fats in the food.

But then what?

After the food has been properly processed, the tongue helps push the bolus into the posterior portion of the oral cavity and into the opening of the pharynx. But isn't there a potential problem here? Doesn't the pharynx open into both the nasal cavity above and into the trachea and esophagus below? Of those three potential paths, two of these are not at all desirable. Obviously, food does not belong in the nose or in the lungs. So, what gives?

Well, when a food bolus enters the pharynx, the soft palate raises up. It makes a seal between the nasal

cavity and the pharynx. The soft palate prevents the bolus from moving up into the nose.

As the muscles of the pharynx contract, the bolus is pushed farther down toward the esophagus. However, as the bolus moves down there are two possible routes it can take, into the trachea or into the esophagus. Well, our Master Designer has that issue handled.

At the level of the larynx is a flap of cartilage called the *epiglottis*. This flap stays open to allow air to pass though the pharynx on its way into the trachea (and thence into the lungs). But as food or drink approaches the level of the larynx, things quickly change. The epiglottis closes over the entrance to the trachea. This keeps food from entering the airway, guiding it instead into the upper portion of the esophagus. (By the way, food entering the airway is called *aspiration*, and it can be a very serious situation if enough food "goes down the wrong way.")

To this point, the act of swallowing is under voluntary control. The muscles involved so far have

TAKING A CLOSER LOOK
Swallowing

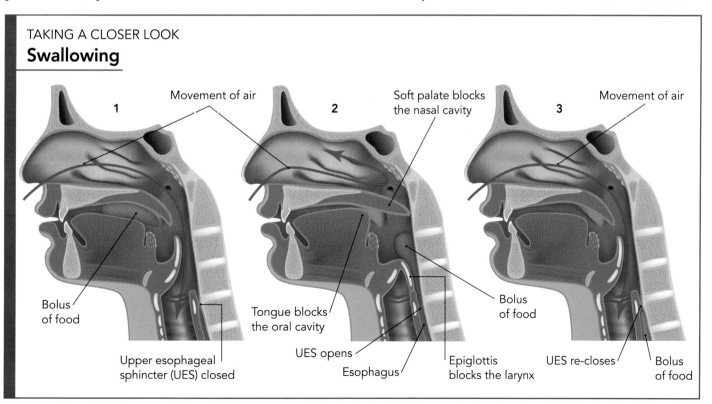

1 — Movement of air — Bolus of food — Upper esophageal sphincter (UES) closed

2 — Soft palate blocks the nasal cavity — Tongue blocks the oral cavity — UES opens — Esophagus — Epiglottis blocks the larynx

3 — Movement of air — Bolus of food — UES re-closes — Bolus of food

been skeletal muscle. Frankly, this makes perfect sense, doesn't it? You actively begin the process of swallowing. It is something you *intend* to do. However, after you begin to swallow, the remainder of this process is involuntary. You don't have to think about pushing food into the stomach. It sort of *just happens.*

But remember that below the upper third of the esophagus, the muscle in its wall changes into a mixture of smooth and skeletal muscle and then into smooth muscle exclusively. Thanks to the types of muscle God used in designing the esophagus, it is up to you to decide when to swallow something. Once the process has begun, however, the automatic wave-like contractions of the esophagus's smooth muscle components complete the job of transporting your food to your stomach.

When the food bolus enters the esophagus, an interesting phenomenon occurs. It is called peristalsis. *Peristalsis* is a series of coordinated movements of the muscles along the length of a tube, like the esophagus. This sequence of contraction and relaxation is what moves the swallowed material down the esophagus and into the stomach. As the food nears the stomach, the lower esophageal sphincter relaxes to allow food to enter the stomach. This muscle movement along the esophagus has been described as being like a "wave." Peristalsis is controlled by nerve centers in the medulla oblongata. Therefore, you do not have to think about making the muscles in the walls of your esophagus or intestines move in a coordinated wave-like pattern to move material along. Thanks to this fine design, peristalsis *"just happens."*

Peristalsis is another amazing design feature of the human body. It is hard to imagine that the precise patterns in which smooth muscle in the esophagus are laid out *just happened!* It is hard to imagine that the nerve inputs from the swallowing center in the medulla found their way to precisely the right places

along the esophagus *randomly!* We can be thankful God made it that way.

Peristalsis also happens throughout the GI tract, as well as in other tubular structures, such as the ureters. Without peristalsis, which goes on without you giving it a thought, the food you eat would never move on through your digestive tract. It is another example of an incredible Designer using similar designs in multiple places in the body.

The Stomach

After food passes through the gastroesophageal sphincter, it enters an enlarged region of the GI tract called the stomach. Most people think of the stomach merely as a place where stomach acids break down food. This view is very oversimplified, as we shall soon see.

Not only does the stomach secrete acid, it churns and mixes food to aid in digestion. Further, the stomach acts as a holding chamber for food being processed. This allows food to be delivered to the small intestine a little at a time, in manageable quantities.

In the average person, the stomach, when empty, is about 20 centimeters (about 8 inches) long and contains less than 60 milliliters (roughly two ounces) of fluid. However, after a very large meal, the very

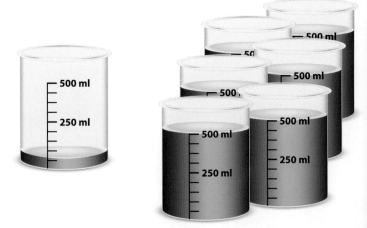

60 milliliters   3 liters

stretchable stomach can expand to accommodate around 3 liters!

Anatomy of the Stomach

The stomach is located in the left upper quadrant of the abdomen. It lies just below the diaphragm and is anterior to (in front of) the pancreas. It looks like a large curved bag. The lateral aspect of the stomach is called the *greater curvature*. This is entirely logical as it is a big curve. The medial aspect of the stomach is a smaller curve. This is known as the *lesser curvature*.

When empty, the stomach lining looks wrinkled, having lots of folds. These folds are called *rugae*. Rugae allow for the expansion of the stomach as it fills with food.

The stomach itself is composed of four main regions: the cardia, the fundus, the body, and the pyloris.

The proximal portion of the stomach — the part nearest the entry of the esophagus — is called the *cardia*. Think of the word "cardiac" here. This part of the stomach is near the heart. It is here where the esophagus empties into the stomach.

Next is the *fundus*. This is the domed-shaped portion of the stomach lateral to (to the side of) the cardia.

Next comes the *body* of the stomach. This is the largest of the four regions and is made up of the central portion of the organ.

Finally, we come to the *pyloris*. This region of the stomach empties into the proximal portion of the small intestine. The pyloris itself is often thought

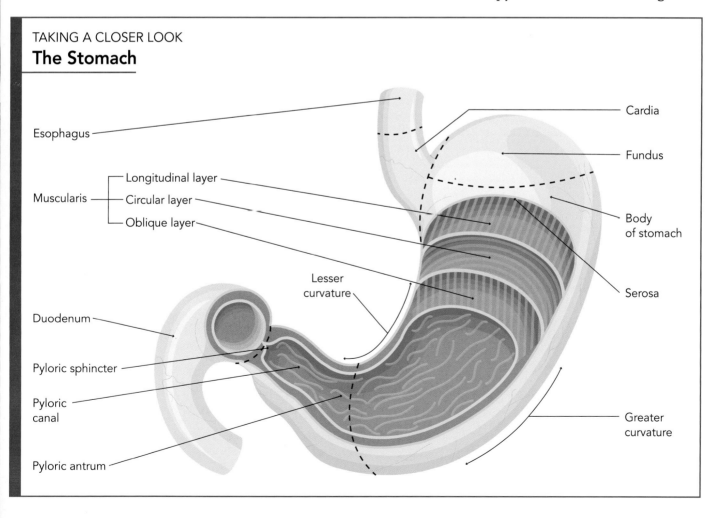

TAKING A CLOSER LOOK
The Stomach

Esophagus

Muscularis — Longitudinal layer
Circular layer
Oblique layer

Duodenum

Pyloric sphincter

Pyloric canal

Pyloric antrum

Lesser curvature

Cardia

Fundus

Body of stomach

Serosa

Greater curvature

of as having two parts. The *pyloric antrum* is its wider, larger part, and the *pyloric canal* is the distal, narrower portion.

Just as there are sphincters in the esophagus, the same can be said of the stomach. The emptying of the stomach into the small intestine is controlled by the *pyloric sphincte*r. This sphincter is located at the junction of the stomach and the small intestine.

Blood Supply of the Stomach

The arterial blood supply of the stomach comes primarily from branches of the *celiac trunk*, a branch of the abdominal aorta. The lesser curvature of the stomach is supplied by the *right* and *left gastric arterie*s. The greater curvature of the stomach gets its arterial blood from the *right* and *left gastroepiploic

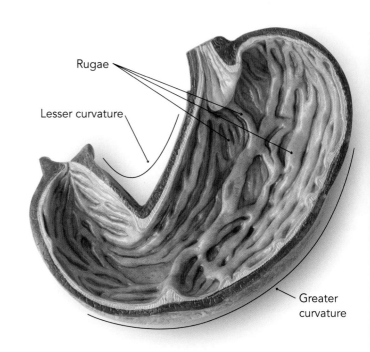

Rugae

Lesser curvature

Greater curvature

The Omentum

You know you have arms and legs, a liver and kidneys, a stomach and a mouth. But did you know that God equipped you with an apron? This apron is inside your abdomen. The Latin word for "apron" is *omentum*. The omentum — actually you have two, a *greater omentum* and a *lesser omentum* — is a double fold of peritoneal membrane. The greater omentum looks like an apron. It contains blood vessels, and a fair amount of fat is deposited in it.

The greater omentum is hooked onto the duodenum and the stomach's greater curvature. It drops from there down into the lower abdomen and pelvis. Then it folds backward and continues back up to anchor onto the transverse colon. This apron is thus draped over the organs of the abdomen. The much smaller lesser omentum is more like a small curtain between the liver and the lesser curvature of the stomach.

The greater omentum is called the "policeman of the abdomen." Because the omentum is large, thin, slippery, and loose, it is able to insinuate itself into lots of nooks and crannies in your abdomen and pelvis. And if an infection or any other sort of inflammation gets started, the omentum sort of sticks to it, allowing the infection-fighting cells in your blood stream quick access to the place and limiting the spread of infection. The idea of calling the greater omentum the abdomen's policeman came from a British surgeon named Rutherford Morrison, back in 1906. He said it was sort of like a jellyfish whose tentacles quietly reached "wherever mischief was brewing" (*British Medical Journal* 1:76, 1906), such as in near an inflamed appendix. Like the appendix, the omentum can be surgically removed and you can go on to live without it just fine. But God designed it for a purpose, and as long as you have it, it helps protect you.

arteries (sometimes called *gastroomental arteries* because they also supply blood to the *omentum* — a large apron-like fold of the peritoneal lining that is draped over the front of the abdominal organs).

Venous drainage of the stomach is by way of the *right* and *left gastric veins*, as well as the *right* and *left gastroepiploic veins* (sometimes called the *gastroomental veins*).

Functions of the Stomach

The stomach is not just an organ designed to make acid, although it does do that quite well. As we examine the mucosa of the stomach in greater detail, you will appreciate just how extraordinary this organ is. Let's get started.

The mucosal layer of the stomach has, at its surface, a layer of special epithelial cells called *mucous cells*. As you might imagine, these cells secrete mucus. These mucous cells are found throughout the entire lining of the stomach. Mucus is very, very important. Have you ever wondered how the stomach protects itself? After all, the stomach secretes a lot of acid, and this acid is there to help digest the food we eat. Why does the stomach then not digest itself? Well, that's where the mucus comes in.

The mucus made by all those mucous cells protects the stomach lining from the corrosive effects of the very powerful acid in the stomach. First of all, the mucus provides a barrier between the acid and the epithelial cells of the mucosa. It keeps the acid from directly touching the stomach lining. This layer of mucus is thick and makes a good barrier.

TAKING A CLOSER LOOK
The Stomach Lining

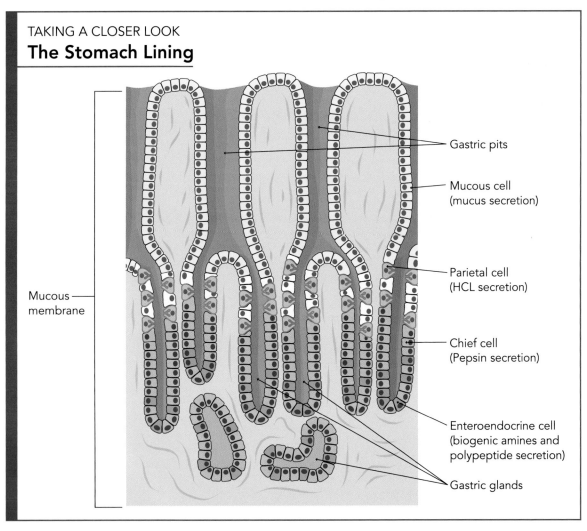

Gastric pits

Mucous cell (mucus secretion)

Parietal cell (HCL secretion)

Chief cell (Pepsin secretion)

Enteroendocrine cell (biogenic amines and polypeptide secretion)

Gastric glands

Mucous membrane

Furthermore, this mucous layer contains a large amount of bicarbonate — a chemical found in baking soda — which neutralizes the acid near the stomach lining.

A closer examination of the stomach lining reveals thousands and thousands of small pits that extend down into the mucosal layer. These pits are called *gastric pits*. While the upper portion of these pits is lined exclusively by mucous cells, farther down there are many different types of cells. These deeper regions of the gastric pits are called *gastric glands*.

The different cell types in the gastric glands are the reason the stomach is able to perform many different

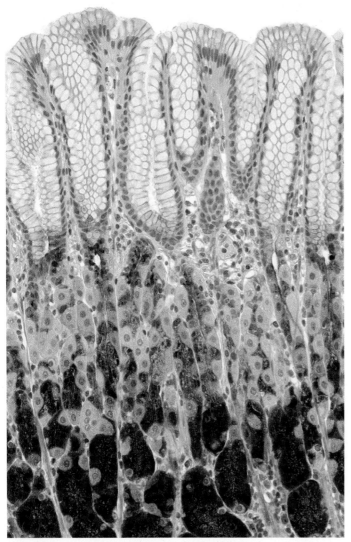

Pepsinogen enzymes in stomach glands (brown)

Proenzymes

Enzymes are proteins that increase the rate of chemical reactions. As you might expect, in something as complex as the human body, there are hundreds of different enzymatic reactions needed to maintain its proper function.

However, not all enzymes are alike. Some enzymes are active the instant they are produced. Other enzymes are made in an initial, inactive form called a proenzyme.

We have already seen an example of this, namely, pepsinogen. Pepsinogen is the proenzyme of the enzyme pepsin. Pepsinogen is inactive when produced in the chief cells and has no activity until it is secreted into the stomach. When it comes into contact with hydrochloric acid in the stomach, it is converted into pepsin. Pepsin then begins breaking down proteins.

So why is this such a great design? If pepsinogen were an active enzyme, it would begin to break down proteins right away, even before being secreted into the stomach. The proteins it would attack would be the proteins in the chief cells that produce it! The proteins in the chief cells themselves would be damaged. Not an ideal situation at all, right? The only way this could work is that a proenzyme is made first, then the pro-enzyme is taken to where it is needed. Then, and only then, is it activated.

So once again you must ask yourself, could something like this be the result of chance? How could an inactive enzyme evolve all by itself, an enzyme of no use at all prior to its activation in another location? Could random processes occurring over millions of years result in a system so finely tuned as this, with exactly the right thing happening in exactly the right place at exactly the right time? This could only be the handi-work of our marvelous Master Designer!

We will see other examples of this as we continue our exploration of the human body.

functions. Perhaps the most important of these is the *parietal cell*. Found along the walls of the gastric gland, parietal cells secrete hydrochloric acid (HCl). This powerful acid begins breaking down food.

Chief cells are found in the lower regions of gastric glands. These cells produce a substance called pepsinogen. Pepsinogen really does not do anything. However, when pepsinogen is produced by the chief cells and is then released into the acidic environment of the stomach, it is converted into *pepsin*. Pepsin is an active enzyme that breaks down proteins into smaller components. This is a very important step in the digestion of the food we eat. The chief cells also produce *lipase,* which help break down fats in our food.

By the way, there are a lot of biochemical substances with "-ogen" at the end of their names, like pepsinogen. This suffix means that the word refers to a chemical pre-cursor for an active chemical.

In addition to the parietal cells and chief cells, there are other cell types that produce some very important, and very specialized, substances. One of these substances is *gastrin*, a hormone that aids in stimulating acid production in the stomach.

One last thing to mention here is something that has nothing to do with digesting food, but it is very, very important nevertheless. It is called *intrinsic factor*, a special type of protein made by parietal cells. Intrinsic factor is vital to the body because, without it, vitamin B12 cannot be absorbed. You see, vitamin B12 must bind to intrinsic factor in the stomach in order to be later absorbed in the small intestine. Without adequate amounts of vitamin B12, the body cannot produce mature red blood cells, and a person can become dangerously anemic. This particular type of anemia is known as *pernicious anemia*.

Control of Stomach Acid Secretion

On any given day, the stomach produces between two and three liters of acid. That's a lot of very corrosive stuff to have in the stomach. Is this acid made around the clock? No, not at all. Stomach acid secretion is regulated and controlled by several mechanisms.

First of all, to a certain degree, stomach acid secretion is regulated by the senses and mind. Just as saliva production can be triggered by the mere sight or smell of food, stomach acid production can be, also. This type of nervous system control mechanism — the result of smelling, seeing, or thinking about food — often starts the process of acid stimulation.

Next, as food enters the stomach, the walls of the stomach are stretched. Special receptors in the stomach are triggered by this stretching, and the receptors send signals to the brain. In the brain, these signals are processed, and a response is sent, instructing the stomach to produce more acid.

Phases of Gastric Secretion

PHASE	STIMULI	PATHWAY
Cephalic (stimulate)	Sight, smell, taste or thought of food	1) Vagus (M3 receptors) 2) Histamine (H2 receptor) 3) Gastrin
Gastric (stimulate)	Food in the stomach	1) Stretch: local reflex (M3 receptors) 2) Chemical substances in food (gastrin) 3) Increase pH: Inhibition of somatostatin (GHIH) release
Intestinal (inhibit)	Chyme in the duodenum	

Pernicious Anemia

Anemia is a condition in which either the quantity or quality of a person's red blood cells is poor. Since the hemoglobin in red blood cells carries oxygen to all parts of your body, anemia can cause a person to be pale and weak. There are many causes of anemia, and treatment involves treating the underlying problem. Some forms of anemia are caused by a deficiency of the raw materials needed to make healthy red blood cells. These raw materials include iron and vitamin B12.

Pernicious anemia is a type of anemia associated with a deficiency of vitamin B12. This lack of vitamin B12 is most often the result of inadequate *intrinsic factor* production by the parietal cells in the stomach. Whenever you eat food containing vitamin B12, such as meat, eggs, dairy products, or nuts, intrinsic factor binds to the vitamin B12 in the stomach. This makes it possible to absorb this important vitamin later, near the end of the small intestine. Without intrinsic factor, vitamin B12 cannot be properly absorbed.

Symptoms of pernicious anemia are in many ways similar to other anemias. The patient may have varying degrees of fatigue, shortness of breath with exertion, and pale skin. In addition, patients with pernicious anemia often suffer numbness and tingling in the hands and feet and complain of a sore tongue. These are neurological symptoms associated with a lack a vitamin B12.

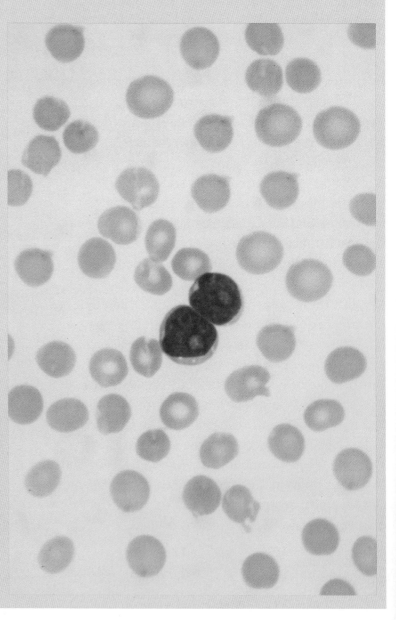

Causes of pernicious anemia include anything that reduces the amount of intrinsic factor produced by the stomach. Illnesses that damage the parietal cells will decrease intrinsic factor production. Surgical procedures in which most or all of the stomach is removed will obviously lead to loss of intrinsic factor production, and thus loss of vitamin B12 absorption.

The body cannot produce vitamin B12 on its own. So, in situations where it cannot be absorbed, vitamin B12 must be provided directly to the body. Treatment for pernicious anemia is administration of vitamin B12. This is usually accomplished by regular intramuscular injections of the important vitamin. As you might guess from the name *pernicious*, this sort of anemia can be very dangerous if untreated, and before the invention of injectable vitamin B12, people sometimes died of the disease.

There are also chemical triggers for acid production. The presence of partially digested food in the stomach can stimulate a cell called a *G cell*. When stimulated, this G cell produces a hormone called *gastrin*. Gastrin then stimulates the parietal cells to produce more stomach acid.

Is stomach acid production ever slowed down or inhibited? Yes! We would not want stomach acid production to continue unchecked, would we?

In situations where the stomach acid level is very high, the production of gastrin is decreased. When gastrin levels go down, the stimulation of stomach acid production goes down. This helps keep acid levels from getting too high.

Acid production is also decreased when the stomach's contents empty into the small intestine. When acidic material is detected in the duodenum, stomach acid production is reduced.

Motility of the Stomach

In addition to its secretory activities, the stomach has other functions. It serves as a holding and mixing chamber.

The stomach can expand to accommodate a significant amount of food during and after a meal. In fact, food generally remains in the stomach between two and four hours. Meals rich in carbohydrates (sugars and starches) tend to pass

Vomiting

Vomiting is the forceful emptying of the contents of the stomach through the mouth. This very unpleasant experience is familiar to nearly everyone.

Vomiting (or *emesis*) results from sudden, forceful contraction of the muscles of the abdomen and the diaphragm. This muscle contraction results in an increase in intraabdominal pressure. This pressure increase, along with relaxation of the gastroesophageal sphincter, results in the contents of the stomach being forced up through the esophagus and out the mouth.

Vomiting results from the processing of sensory inputs to the vomiting (or emetic) center in the medulla. Nerve signals are then sent to initiate vomiting.

Many things can trigger vomiting. It may be something as simple as a bad smell or the sight of blood. Emesis can result from illness, food poisoning, an adverse reaction to some kinds of medications, chemotherapy, radiation therapy, severe stress, motion sickness, or pregnancy, among other things.

Vomiting often goes away by itself. But ongoing vomiting, besides being utterly miserable, can cause dehydration, which might require intravenous fluids. Medications to combat nausea and vomiting are called *anti-emetics*. Anti-emetics are often used to make people feel better and stop vomiting until the underlying cause of the vomiting is treated or resolved on its own.

Peptic Ulcer Disease

Peptic ulcer disease (PUD) occurs when there is damage to the epithelial lining of either the stomach or duodenum. These damaged areas are most often referred to as ulcers. If the ulcer is in the stomach, it is called a *gastric ulcer*. If it is in the duodenum, it is called a *duodenal ulcer*. Peptic ulcer disease is very common and is estimated to occur in about 5 percent of the U.S. population.

This illness often presents feelings of "indigestion" — an uncomfortable burning sensation in the upper abdomen. For some patients, the discomfort occurs *after* eating. With other patients, the discomfort lessens *with* eating. Vomiting, even the vomiting of blood, may occur with PUD. Poor appetite and loss of weight are also frequent symptoms.

Peptic ulcer disease is common in people who regularly take non-steroidal anti-inflammatory medication (NSAIDs). These drugs are often used to minimize the discomfort associated with arthritis. NSAIDs also have the unfortunate side effect of damaging the lining of the stomach and duodenum, leading to irritation and ulceration.

PUD is also associated with the presence of the bacteria *Helicobacter pylori* (or *H. pylori*). *H. pylori* is able to survive in the harsh environment in the stomach by producing substances to protect itself from the stomach acid. Unfortunately, the mechanisms that protect the bacteria also harm the epithelial cells of the stomach lining. This can lead to ulcer formation. However (isn't there always a "however" . . .), *H. pylori* does not *always* lead to PUD. In fact, it has been estimated that up to half the world's population has *H. pylori* colonization in their GI tracts. The majority of these people (about 90 percent) will never have peptic ulcer disease. On the other hand, roughly 70 percent of people with PUD have stomach irritation due to *H. pylori*. So how do you know whether asymptomatic people (those with no symptoms) need to be treated for their *H. pylori*? Obviously, this is an area of very active medical research.

Amazingly, at this time there appears to be no link between diet and PUD. There are really no foods that directly increase a person's risk of developing a gastric or duodenal ulcer. Although there is continuing debate on this, there has been no clear evidence that smoking or alcohol consumption increases the risk for PUD.

Treatment of PUD includes the cessation of NSAIDs and administration of medications that lower stomach acid production. Antibiotic treatment for *H. pylori* infection, if present, is also very important and has been shown to reduce recurrence of the disease. In recent years, surgery for PUD is uncommon. However, on rare occasions it is needed to repair an ulcer which extends through the entire wall of the GI tract (a so-called *perforated ulcer*) or when the ulcer causes severe, uncontrolled bleeding.

Helicobacter pylori bacteria (pink)

though the stomach more rapidly than meals high in protein. Thus, the stomach acts as a holding chamber as its processed contents are gradually emptied into the small intestine.

Furthermore, the muscle activity of the stomach helps mix and grind the food as digestion continues. Coordinated muscle contractions in the stomach also propel the food along its course toward the pyloric sphincter and into the small intestine.

And Now . . .

And now we are going to put a hold on our journey through the GI tract, at least for a short time. It's time to introduce the three remaining accessory digestive organs: the pancreas, the liver, and the gallbladder. Each of these organs makes vital contributions to the digestive processes, once the milkshake-like mixture of partially digested food is allowed to exit the stomach through the pyloric sphincter. Therefore, we will digress from the digestive tract and examine these accessory organs.

The Pancreas

The pancreas is an accessory digestive organ that is located behind the stomach. The pancreas is relatively small, only about 15 centimeters (6 inches) long. However, it has a lot of very big jobs.

The pancreas functions in the digestive system as an *exocrine gland* — this is a gland that works by secreting its product into a duct. The pancreas also functions as an *endocrine gland*, a gland that secretes its products directly into the bloodstream. In other volumes of *Wonders of the Human Body*, you will learn about its role as an endocrine gland and the hormone it produces. At this time, we will concentrate on the pancreas's role in the digestive process.

Gross Anatomy of the Pancreas

The *head* of the pancreas is nestled in the curve of the duodenum. The *body* of the pancreas extends laterally from the head, and it tapers into a *tail*.

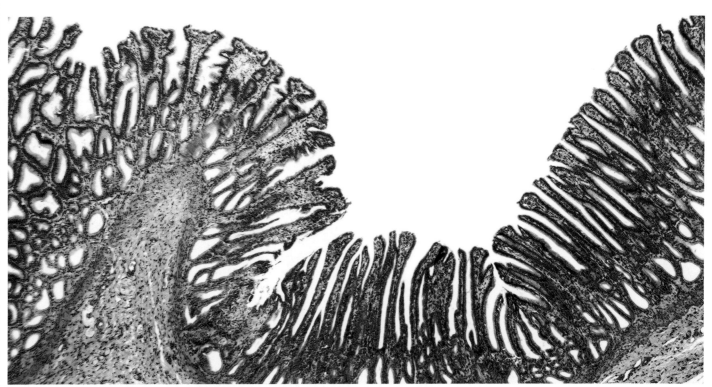

Image of the fundus, which is the enlarged area at the top of the stomach

Why Do We Burp?

Burping (also called "belching," or "eructation" if you want to impress your friends) is the result of swallowing air. We swallow air in small amounts as we eat, drink, and swallow the saliva in our mouths to avoid drooling. This air, as you might expect, rises to the top in our stomach fluids. When a bubble of air puts pressure on the upper part of the stomach, it triggers a reflex through the vagus nerve. This reflex causes the sphincter between the esophagus and stomach to relax, allowing the air to enter the lower esophagus. The presence of an air bubble in the lower esophagus triggers two more reflex responses, one controlled by the vagus nerve and another through the spinal cord. The spinal reflex causes a reverse of the wave-like peristalsis that is triggered when we swallow, propelling the air bubble up the esophagus toward the throat. The vagus nerve reflex relaxes the muscles controlling the opening between the esophagus and pharynx, opening the way for the upward-moving air to escape. The "burp" sound is produced by rapid air movement through the pharynx.

This sort of burp is called a *gastric belch* and is a normal occurrence, ordinarily happening at least 20–25 times a day to vent the air in the stomach. The vagal nerve reflexes that make the gastric belch happen are mediated by the area postrema in the brain's medulla. Vomiting is largely managed by the same region of the brain, which makes sense when you realize the vomiting involves the forceful expulsion of stomach contents other than air.

Burping can be worsened by drinking soda, which contains carbon dioxide that is released in the stomach. Rarely, people with ulcers or gallbladder disease may experience an increase in burping as part of their symptoms.

There is another kind of burp that has nothing to do with the stomach. It is called a *supragastric belch*. (*Supra* means "above," as in "above the stomach.") In a supragastric belch, the air ultimately forced across the pharynx does not come up from the stomach. It is instead forcibly drawn into the upper esophagus. This is done by relaxing the diaphragm to lower the pressure inside the chest cavity while simultaneously coordinating pharyngeal muscles with muscles at the base of the tongue to open the esophagus to air. Air is thus sucked into the upper esophagus. Then the air is forced back out, producing the characteristic "burp" sound. Some people do this when under stress, and in some people, this sort of behavior becomes a bad habit.

At the end of the day, you will find that when you burp is far more important than why you burp. Bad (or at least, not good) times would include while the pastor is preaching, during Thanksgiving dinner at your grandmother's house, or during your Nobel Prize acceptance speech. Happily, burping is managed by a combination of reflexive and voluntary controls.

The pancreas empties its secretory products through ducts into the duodenum, which is part of the small intestine. (We'll learn a lot more about it later.) The *pancreatic duct* runs through the length of the pancreas and then joins another duct — the *common bile duct* — which carries substances produced in the liver. These ducts merge just before emptying into the duodenum, forming the *hepatopancreatic ampulla* (often called the *ampulla of Vater*). Its long name describes the origins of the substances it carries: *hepato-* for liver and *-pancreatic* for pancreas. *Ampulla* is Latin for "flask." In anatomy, an *ampulla* is a sac-like enlargement of a tubular structure. You've probably seen pictures of flasks in laboratories, so you can picture the ampulla of Vater as it holds important digestive juices and empties them into the duodenum. This ampulla is named for the 18th-century German anatomist who discovered it, Abraham Vater.

Several important sphincters regulate the flow of digestive juices through this highway of ducts. The *sphincter of Oddi* — discovered by the 19th-century Italian anatomist Ruggero Oddi — controls their entry into the duodenum. This muscular valve also ensures that the contents of the duodenum do not back up into the ampulla. The sphincter of Oddi holds back digestive juices pooling in the ampulla of Vater until signaled by the hormone cholecystokinin to relax and open.

Many people have a second pancreatic duct called the *accessory duct* or the *duct of Santorini*. As you've probably already guessed, this accessory — meaning "extra" — duct was discovered early in the 18th century by an Italian anatomist, Giovanni Domenico Santorini. This duct usually empties directly into the duodenum, though in some people, it simply joins the pancreatic duct as it courses through the pancreas.

TAKING A CLOSER LOOK
The Pancreas

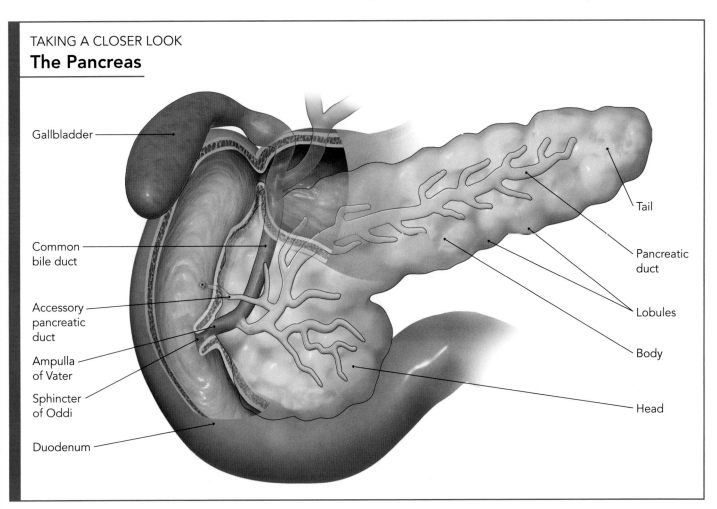

TAKING A CLOSER LOOK
The Pancreatic Acini

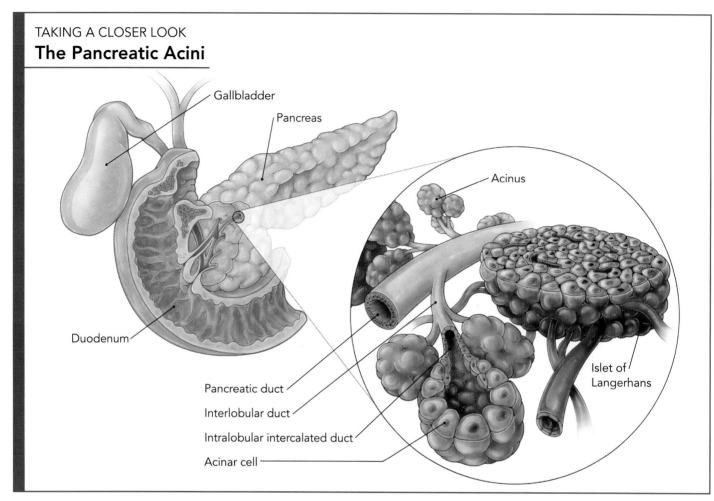

Why do some people have an accessory duct and some do not? Why does the accessory duct not always empty the same way? Well, all human embryos have an accessory duct because the pancreas is formed from two parts that fuse together. Each part has a duct. As the embryo grows and the parts of the pancreas fuse, the organ's "plumbing" arranges itself so that the main duct takes over most or all of the drainage, and the accessory duct that was very important early on often closes because it is not needed anymore.

While the main anatomical features of the human body are mostly the same in everyone, there is a fair amount of variability in some of the details. Think about it. Faces look different. So why not the internal anatomy, too? This is a good example. Surgeons and *gastroenterologists* (doctors specializing in the GI tract) must know the usual anatomy very well while,

at the same time being alert for all the known and as yet unknown variations that occur. Some of these variations can be difficult to spot when operating or exploring diseased or blocked ducts with fiber-optic instruments. No one wants to inadvertently damage a tiny structure just because he or she did not know it was there!

Microscopic Anatomy of the Pancreas

The microscopic structure of the pancreas is quite fascinating. The majority of the pancreas consists of clusters of cells called *acini*. These are groups of secretory cells clustered around a small duct. These cells secrete their products into the tiny duct. These secretions combine to form *pancreatic juice*. The small ducts connect with many other ducts and empty into the pancreatic and accessory

Pancreatitis

Pancreatitis is a very serious medical condition in which the pancreas is inflamed. It is characterized by abdominal pain, mostly in the upper abdomen. The pain often radiates to the back. The pain from pancreatitis can range from mild to very severe. Nausea, vomiting, and often fever accompany the abdominal pain.

Pancreatitis can be life threatening. When the pancreas is inflamed, the proenzymes leak from the secretory cells and, when activated, begin digesting proteins — any proteins they encounter. These protein-digesting enzymes begin to damage the pancreas itself. You might say that the pancreas tries to digest itself. Obviously, this is a very bad situation.

One of most common causes of pancreatitis is gallstones. Gallstones can cause pancreatitis by obstructing the pancreatic duct. This obstruction prevents the pancreas from emptying properly, and the pressure in the pancreatic duct increases. This results in damage to the pancreatic cells and triggers the breakdown of pancreatic tissue.

Prolonged alcohol use can damage the pancreas and lead to pancreatitis. Other causes of pancreatitis include high levels of fats in the blood, high levels of calcium in the blood, cystic fibrosis, infections, trauma, and certain medications.

Treatment of pancreatitis includes pain medication and intravenous fluids. Production of pancreatic juice is stimulated by the entry of stomach acid mixed with food into the duodenum. Therefore, during the initial stages of treatment, the patient is usually given nothing to eat or drink in order to reduce the inflammation by letting the pancreas rest. Treatment of any underlying cause is also important, whether this is removing an obstructing gallstone, treating an infection, or discontinuing an offending medication. In rare situations, the pancreas becomes so damaged that surgery is required to remove part of the gland.

ducts. Eventually, the pancreatic juice finds its way into the duodenum — the first part of the small intestine — where it makes its contribution to the digestive process. So, you see, in this way, the pancreas is functioning as an exocrine gland. Other cells in the pancreas, called *pancreatic islets* or *islets of Langerhans*, produce the hormones that give the pancreas its endocrine functions. Hormones do not enter the ducts but instead go into the bloodstream. Again, more about this later.

Around 1,500 milliliters (1.6 quarts) of pancreatic juice is produced each day. It is made up of water, bicarbonate, and digestive enzymes. The bicarbonate in the pancreatic juice helps neutralize the acid in the stomach contents that empty into the duodenum. This lowering of the acid level helps protect the lining of the duodenum as well as assuring the proper environment for the function of the digestive enzymes.

There are various digestive enzymes in the pancreatic juice, and they perform many functions. The enzyme *amylase* breaks down starches. *Lipases* break down lipids (fats). Nucleic acids are digested by *ribonuclease* and *deoxyribonuclease*. It seems like there is an enzyme to break down pretty much anything that finds its way into the duodenum.

Pancreatic acini utilize proenzymes to safely produce protein-digesting enzymes. The secretory cells in the acini produce trypsinogen and chymotrypsinogen to digest proteins. Just as in the stomach, these enzymes cannot be made in the acini as active enzymes. If they were active, the acini would digest themselves. These proenzymes are delivered into the duodenum where they are converted into their active forms. In this case, trypsinogen is converted to *trypsin* and *chymotrypsinogen* is converted to chymotrypsin.

Blood Supply of the Pancreas

The arterial blood supply of the pancreas comes from the *celiac* and *superior mesenteric arteries,* two major branches of the abdominal aorta. The celiac trunk branches into several large arteries. One of these — the splenic artery — supplies the body and tail of the pancreas with arterial blood on its way to the spleen. (The spleen is located near the tail of the pancreas.) Another branch of the celiac trunk supplies blood to the liver, the stomach, the duodenum, and the head of the pancreas. The head of the pancreas receives an additional arterial blood supply from a branch of the superior mesenteric artery, the second major branch of the abdominal aorta. Venous drainage of the pancreas is primarily via the *splenic vein.*

Pancreatic Cancer

Pancreatic cancer is an all too common disease in our world today. In the United States, it is presently one of the leading causes of cancer deaths.

The most common form of this disease is called adenocarcinoma of the pancreas. This type of cancer begins in the pancreatic cells that produce digestive enzymes. It is a very aggressive form of cancer. In many patients, by the time any symptoms occur, the cancer has already spread to other organs of the body. For this reason, survival rates for adenocarcinoma of the pancreas are very low. Only about 5 percent live for five years after diagnosis.

Risk factors for pancreatic cancer include smoking (again, please, please, never start smoking!), diabetes, and obesity.

CANCER TYPE	ESTIMATED NEW 2018 CASES	ESTIMATED 2018 DEATHS
Lung and Bronchus	234,030	154,050
Colon and Rectal	140,250	50,630
Pancreatic	55,440	44,330
Breast	268,670	41,400
Liver and Intrahepatic Bile Duct	42,220	30,200
Prostate	164,690	29,430
Leukemia (All Types)	60,300	24,370
Non-Hodgkin Lymphoma	74,680	19,910
Bladder	81,190	17,240
Kidney (Renal Cell and Renal Pelvis) Cancer	65,340	14,970
Endometrial	63,230	11,350
Melanoma	91,270	9,320
Thyroid	53,990	2,060

Ranked by estimated deaths in 2018, American Cancer Society, 2018

The Liver and Gallbladder

In the right upper quadrant of the abdomen is found the largest organ in the digestive system, the liver. Weighing in at about 1.5 kilograms (roughly 3 pounds), the liver is the largest gland in the body.

The liver is positioned just below the diaphragm on the right side of the abdomen. Anteriorly, it is covered almost entirely by the rib cage. It is no accident that an organ as important as the liver is given a place where it can be protected. You see, God thinks of everything.

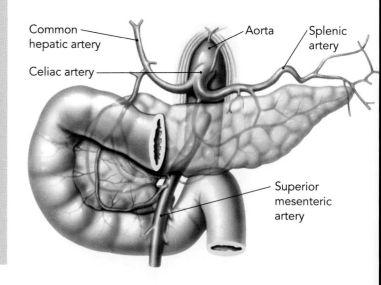

Common hepatic artery

Aorta

Splenic artery

Celiac artery

Superior mesenteric artery

The liver consists of four lobes, only two of which can be seen from a frontal view. Anteriorly, you see a larger *right lobe* and a smaller *left lobe*. These two lobes are separated by the fused membranes of a mesentery called the *falciform ligament*.

From a posterior view, the *caudate lobe* is seen superiorly. Inferiorly, near the gall bladder, is the *quadrate lobe*.

The gallbladder is found near the inferior border of the left lobe of the liver. The gallbladder consists of a rounded *fundus* inferiorly, a central region called the *body*, and the more tapered section superiorly, called the *neck*. From the neck of the gallbladder runs the *cystic duct*. The cystic duct joins the common hepatic duct to form the *common bile duct*.

The Liver — A Closer Look

Of all the organs in the human body, the microscopic anatomy (or histology) of the liver is perhaps the most fascinating. Since the liver is responsible for an incredible number of processes in the body, it stands to reason that its design would be equally incredible. Some experts have suggested that the liver has almost 500 different functions. As you will see, the liver is more than up to the challenge.

The primary cell type found in the liver is the *hepatocyte*. This cell performs many different jobs. From building different types of proteins to breaking down toxins, the hepatocyte is quite the versatile cell. However, it is more than just the hepatocyte that is important here. It is the specialized arrangement

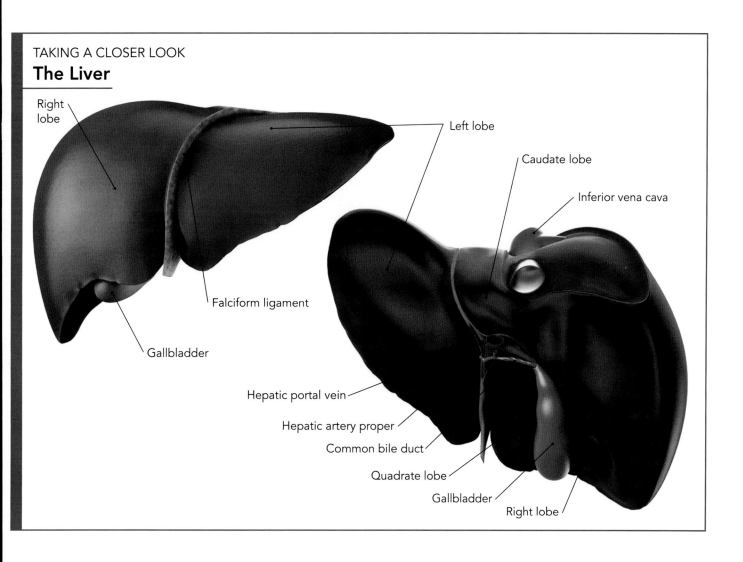

TAKING A CLOSER LOOK
The Liver

Right lobe

Left lobe

Caudate lobe

Inferior vena cava

Falciform ligament

Gallbladder

Hepatic portal vein

Hepatic artery proper

Common bile duct

Quadrate lobe

Gallbladder

Right lobe

in which hepatocytes, along with other important structures, are organized that is so truly remarkable.

Hepatocytes are organized in special units known as *liver lobules*. When viewed under the microscope, these lobules have a hexagonal — six-sided — shape. As with everything else in the human body, the layout of these lobules is no mere accident. The closer you look, the more amazing the design.

In a liver lobule, the hepatocytes are arranged in small plates radiating out from the lobule's center. These projections of hepatocytes are called *hepatic laminae*. These laminae are layers just one cell thick, and they are adjacent to capillaries known as *hepatic sinusoids*. This arrangement gives all the hepatocytes access to lots of blood flow. That proximity to a rich blood supply enables them to do their jobs most effectively, as we will see.

Also, adjacent to these radiating layers of hepatocytes are small ducts called *bile canaliculi*. Into these ducts the hepatocytes secrete a substance called *bile* (hence the name "bile canaliculi"). We will learn more about bile later. As these canaliculi weave their way through the liver lobules, they begin to merge, eventually forming bile ducts. The bile

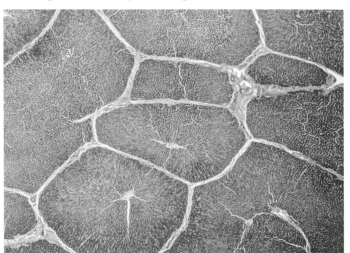

Photomicrograph of liver

TAKING A CLOSER LOOK
Structure of the Liver Lobule

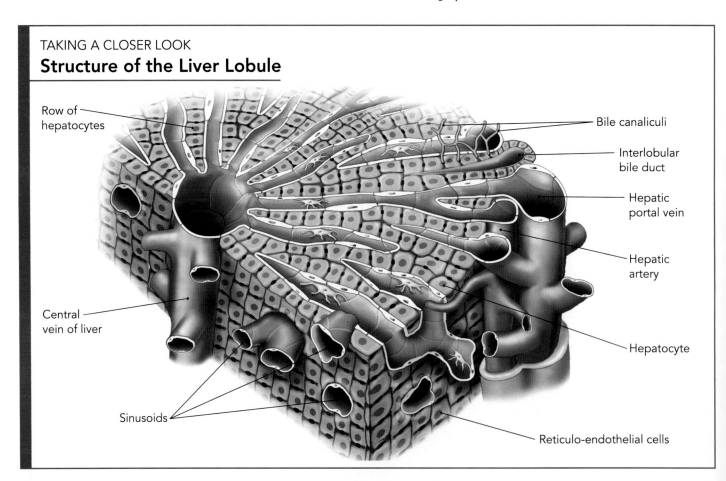

Row of hepatocytes

Bile canaliculi

Interlobular bile duct

Hepatic portal vein

Hepatic artery

Central vein of liver

Hepatocyte

Sinusoids

Reticulo-endothelial cells

ducts merge into ever larger channels resulting in the formation of the *right hepatic duct* and the *left hepatic duct*. Just as the right and left hepatic ducts exit the liver, they merge to form the *common hepatic duct*.

Now turning back to the liver lobules, we find something very interesting at each of the six corners of each hexagonal lobule. Located at each corner is a structure called a *portal triad*. This triad is composed of three things (hence the name *triad*, meaning "three"): a bile duct, a small artery, and a small vein. The bile duct here receives bile from the bile canaliculi previously mentioned. The small artery is a branch of the hepatic artery and brings oxygen-rich blood to the liver. The small vein is a branch of the *portal vein*.

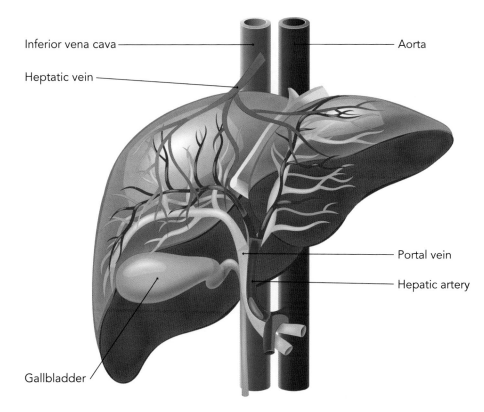

Inferior vena cava — Aorta

Heptatic vein —

Portal vein

Hepatic artery

Gallbladder

Portal Pentad

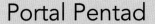

Whenever communicating, it is always best to be as accurate as possible. That being said, the portal triad in the liver is not actually a triad. It is a pentad, meaning it actually contains five things, not just three.

In recent years, it has been determined that the three structures traditionally known to make up a portal triad, well . . . they are not alone. Not only is there a bile duct, a small artery, and a small vein in that "triad" area, but also two other things. The two newly discovered structures are lymphatic vessels and a branch of the vagus nerve. So much for the triad thing, I suppose.

However, in this book we will continue to refer to the area in question as the "portal triad." Somehow, "portal pentad" just doesn't work for me. . . .

Coming directly from the GI tract, venous blood in the portal vein and all its branches is rich in nutrients absorbed from the GI tract, but somewhat lower in oxygen. On arrival at the liver lobules, this venous blood is filtered through the capillary-like hepatic sinusoids, traveling from the lobule's corner to its center. Passing through the sinusoids, the blood delivers lots of nutrients (along with other substances) to the hepatocytes. Ultimately, the hepatic sinusoids empty into the central vein at the center of the liver lobule. The central vein then drains into hepatic veins. From there blood is returned to the heart.

Blood Supply of the Liver

We have previously covered some aspects of the blood supply to the liver, but a more complete description seems prudent here. You see, the blood flowing to the liver comes from two sources, the *portal vein* and the *hepatic artery*. The hepatic artery carries oxygen-rich arterial blood. The portal vein carries nutrient-rich venous blood.

The portal vein brings blood from the GI tract, pancreas, and spleen to the liver. This portal blood carries absorbed nutrients and accounts for about 75 percent of the blood flow to the liver. Interestingly, the portal vein is not really a true vein because it does not take blood to the heart. Instead, it transports blood from the capillary beds in the GI tract to the capillary beds in the liver. This is a great design because it allows the liver to screen the blood from the GI tract for excessive amounts of nutrients and even toxins before the rest of the body is exposed to that blood. The liver removes and processes these materials as needed before sending the portal blood on to the heart to be reoxygenated and returned to the general circulation.

After passing through the liver lobule in hepatic sinusoids, blood from the portal vein empties into *central veins* in the lobule centers. These central veins merge to form *hepatic veins*. The hepatic veins then drain into the inferior vena cava, which takes the blood to the heart.

The Liver's Role in Digestion

One of the primary contributions that the liver makes to the digestive process is the production of a yellow-green liquid known as *bile*. Bile is made up of water, *bile salts*, fats, and *bilirubin*. It is produced continuously during the day and is delivered to the duodenum via the common bile duct. Between meals,

Jaundice

Jaundice is yellowish coloration of the skin due to elevated bilirubin levels. It also can cause discoloration of the sclera (the "whites") of the eyes and even urine.

Jaundice has many causes. It can result from hepatitis, alcoholic liver disease, cirrhosis, or an obstruction of the bile duct by a gallstone or tumor. Situations where red blood cells break down rapidly, such as a hemolytic anemia, can also lead to elevated bilirubin levels. In all these situations, treatment of the underlying problem will hopefully lead to lowering of the bilirubin levels and improvement of the jaundice.

One interesting cause of jaundice occurs in newborns, and it occurs because their livers are not fully mature. This is called *neonatal jaundice*. Neonatal jaundice is most often a benign problem that resolves on its own as liver function matures during the first week or two after birth. A certain amount of bilirubin in the blood is normal, but high levels are not healthy. Therefore, if bilirubin levels are too high, neonatal jaundice is often treated with phototherapy. This involves exposure of the baby's skin to specific wavelengths of light that transform bilirubin molecules into molecules easier for the baby's body to eliminate.

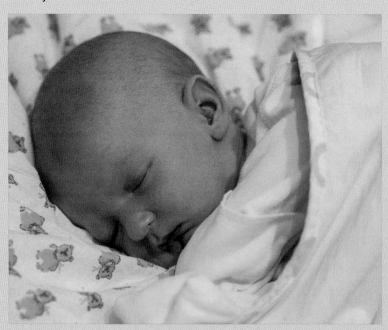

TAKING A CLOSER LOOK
The Relationship Between the Pancreas, Liver, and Duodenum

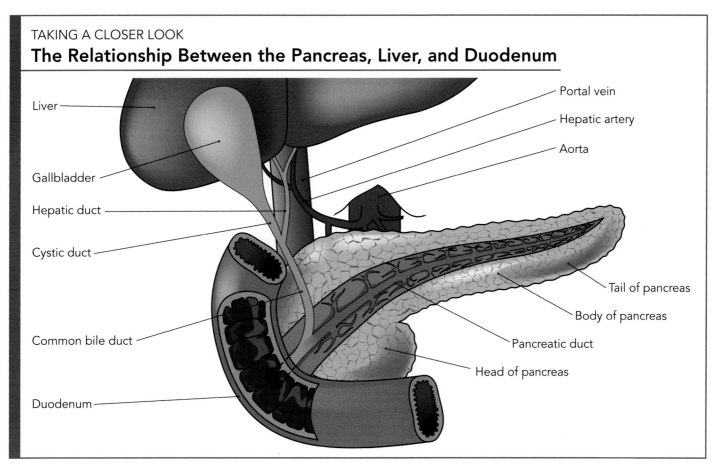

Liver

Gallbladder

Hepatic duct

Cystic duct

Common bile duct

Duodenum

Portal vein

Hepatic artery

Aorta

Tail of pancreas

Body of pancreas

Pancreatic duct

Head of pancreas

when digestive activity is low, the bile is stored in the gallbladder until needed.

Bile makes its way to the intestine through a series of ducts. It leaves the liver through the common hepatic duct. This duct joins the cystic duct, which comes from the gallbladder. Some of the bile goes through the cystic duct to get stored in the gallbladder and later released when needed. The common hepatic duct and the cystic duct, as you see in the illustrations, combine to form the common bile duct. The common bile duct delivers bile to the duodenum.

The bile salts present in bile aid in digestion by helping break down lipids (fats). Fatty substances tend to pass thought the GI tract as droplets (think "globs" of fats and you get the general idea). Bile salts break larger droplets down into smaller droplets. The many smaller droplets have a greater total surface area than fewer, larger droplets. The increased surface area makes it easier for the many

enzymes in the intestine to further break down the fats during digestion.

Bilirubin is the pigment that results in the yellow-green color of bile. It is actually a by-product of the breakdown of red blood cells. As red blood cells age and wear out, they are broken down and recycled. As part of this recycling, bilirubin is produced. The bilirubin is taken up by cells in the liver and then excreted into the bile. After bile is released into the intestine, the bilirubin is broken down into *stercobilin*. Stercobilin is the substance that gives feces its brown color.

Although bilirubin is excreted in the bile and ultimately removed from the body, bile salts have a different fate. Bile salts enter the proximal part of the small intestine (the duodenum) in bile. After doing their job, they are re-absorbed when they arrive in the distal portion of the small intestine (the ileum). They are taken back to the liver and used once again to make bile. The recycling of bile salts is called *enterohepatic circulation*. *Entero-* means "intestine," and *hepatic* means "liver," so this is a good name.

Functions of the Liver

The liver is quite the remarkable organ. As mentioned previously, the liver performs an estimated 500 different functions. It seems only fair that we take some time to explore at least a few of these.

The liver is a primary site for protein metabolism. *Metabolism* refers to all the chemical transformations that happen in our cells, both those that break down biomolecules and those that manufacture them. Thus, protein metabolism refers to the manufacture and break down of proteins and their building blocks, amino acids. As we shall see later,

Hepatitis

Hepatitis is an illness characterized by inflammation of the liver. The major cause of hepatitis is viral infection.

There are, at present, five known major types of viral hepatitis. These are known as Hepatitis A (sometimes called infectious hepatitis), Hepatitis B (also known as serum hepatitis), Hepatitis C, Hepatitis D, and Hepatitis E. Types A and E are spread by ingesting contaminated water or foodstuffs. Hepatitis B, C, and D are spread by contact with infected blood. Of these five types, Hepatitis A and B are the most common.

Symptoms of hepatitis are varied. Some patients have essentially no symptoms, and their disease is detected by abnormalities on blood tests (often when screening for other illnesses). Patients with symptoms might have abdominal pain, nausea, fatigue, and sometimes fever. Frequently, patients will display a yellowish discoloration to the skin and sclera. This is called jaundice.

There are blood tests that are used to screen people for the presence of hepatitis as well as tests used to monitor the function of the liver during the course of the illness.

The majority of people with hepatitis will recover without permanent damage to their liver. Unfortunately, in some patients, the disease progresses quite aggressively. This rapid progression can lead to liver failure and death.

Cases of hepatitis that resolve in less than six months are referred to as *acute hepatitis*. If hepatitis persists for more than six months it is called *chronic hepatitis*. Some patients with more prolonged cases have been successfully treated with special antiviral medications.

TYPE OF HEPATITIS	DESCRIPTION
Hepatitis A	A highly contagious liver infection caused by the hepatitis A virus.
Hepatitis B	A serious liver infection caused by the hepatitis B virus.
Hepatitis C	An infection caused by a virus that attacks the liver and leads to inflammation.
Hepatitis D	A serious liver disease caused by infection with the hepatitis D virus.
Hepatitis E	A liver disease caused by the hepatitis E virus.
Alcoholic hepatitis	Liver inflammation caused by drinking too much alcohol.
Autoimmune hepatitis	Inflammation in the liver that occurs when the immune system attacks the liver.

COMMON FUNCTIONS OF THE LIVER

Production of bile, which helps carry away waste and break down fats in the small intestine during digestion

Production of certain proteins for blood plasma

Production of cholesterol and special proteins to help carry fats through the body

Conversion of excess glucose into glycogen for storage (glycogen can later be converted back to glucose for energy) and to balance and make glucose as needed

Regulation of blood levels of amino acids, which form the building blocks of proteins

Processing of hemoglobin for use of its iron content (the liver stores iron)

Conversion of poisonous ammonia to urea (urea is an end product of protein metabolism and is excreted in the urine)

Clearing the blood of drugs and other poisonous substances

Regulating blood clotting

Resisting infections by making immune factors and removing bacteria from the bloodstream

Clearance of bilirubin, a by-product of the breakdown of red blood cells. If there is an accumulation of bilirubin, the skin and eyes turn yellow.

proteins from our foods are broken down into their component amino acids in the GI tract. Those amino acids can be used by the hepatocytes in the liver to manufacture new proteins, or they can be broken down further to make different kinds of molecules. The liver also manufactures many amino acids, the so-called "non-essential" amino acids. ("Essential" amino acids are those amino acids the body cannot manufacture.)

The liver manufactures most of the proteins found in blood plasma. *Albumin* is the primary protein found in blood plasma, and it is made in the liver. In addition, many of the proteins involved in blood clotting, the so-called *coagulation factors*, are manufactured in the liver. Think about trying to live without these vital proteins. You could bleed to death from a badly skinned knee or a cut finger. Other proteins made in the liver include ceruloplasmin, a protein that transports copper, and thrombopoietin, a protein hormone that regulates the production of platelets.

TAKING A CLOSER LOOK
The Role of the Liver in Metabolism

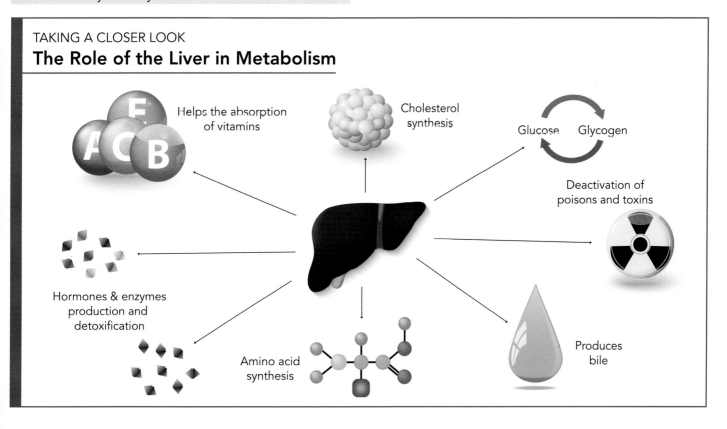

Helps the absorption of vitamins

Cholesterol synthesis

Glucose Glycogen

Deactivation of poisons and toxins

Hormones & enzymes production and detoxification

Amino acid synthesis

Produces bile

Gall Stones

Not uncommonly, people go to their doctor complaining of pain in the right upper quadrant of the abdomen. This "colicky" pain is often described as a bad cramp that radiates to the back, often toward the bottom of the right shoulder blade. This pain is often accompanied by nausea and vomiting.

When this constellation of symptoms occurs, the first diagnosis the doctor thinks about is "gall-stones." Most often, the doctor is correct.

Gallstones are small and almost pebble-like (although to the patient having gallstone pain, they must feel like huge boulders . . .). Most commonly, they are the result of having too much cholesterol or too few bile salts in the bile. After gallstones form, contraction of the gallbladder can result in severe pain.

It has been estimated that up to 20 percent of the population has gallstones. Given that some people have severe pain due to their gallstones, it is amazing that perhaps 80 percent of people with gallstones have no symptoms at all. In fact, it not uncommon to see gallstones on x-ray or ultrasound in a person who is being tested for something totally unre-lated to gall-stone disease.

Treatment for patients having symptoms due to gallstones is most often the surgical removal of the gallbladder.

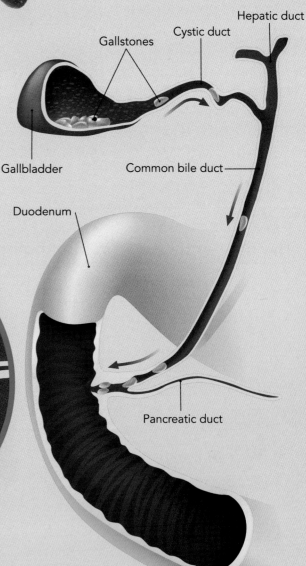

Hepatic duct

Cystic duct

Gallstones

Gallbladder

Common bile duct

Duodenum

Pancreatic duct

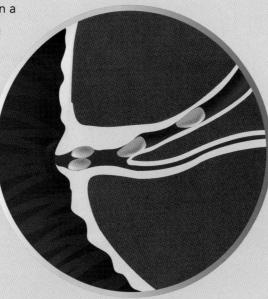

A stone in the common bile duct can block the flow of bile and cause inflammation, infection, and jaundice.

The liver is a site of production and storage of *glycogen*. Glycogen is a storage form of carbohydrates which can easily be broken down into glucose when energy is needed. The liver can also make glucose from amino acids, a process called *gluconeogenesis*. Thus, the liver plays a role in maintaining a normal level of glucose in the blood. This is very important, as glucose is the fuel preferred by the brain.

Cholesterol is a kind of fat molecule your body's cells use to make many hormones. Cholesterol synthesis occurs in the liver. The proteins that carry cholesterol and other fats through the bloodstream are also made in the liver. Transport packages consisting of fat molecules and the protein carrying them are called *lipoproteins*.

The liver is also the site for detoxifying many substances that find their way into the body. An obvious example is alcohol. The liver also helps rid the body of medications, such as penicillin, after they have had their effect in the body. Ammonia, which forms in the intestine when bacteria break down protein, is toxic to the body. Ammonia, delivered to the liver in the portal blood, is converted by the liver into as substance called *urea*. The urea is then safely removed from the body in the urine.

A complete discussion of the amazing abilities of the liver could fill a large textbook. But you get the idea.

The Small Intestine

After passing through the pyloric sphincter, a milkshake-like mixture of partially digested food called *chyme* enters the small intestine. The small intestine is a long tubular structure that seems to wind its way back and forth through the central portion of the abdominal cavity.

TAKING A CLOSER LOOK
The Small Intestines

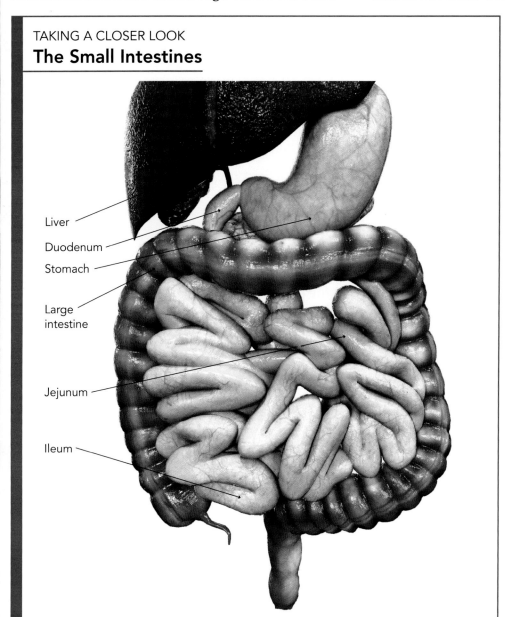

Liver

Duodenum

Stomach

Large intestine

Jejunum

Ileum

Villi from the lining of the small intestine

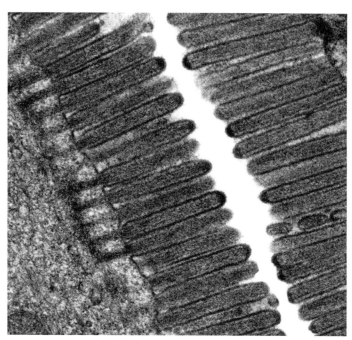

Microvilli of the small intestine

The small intestine is usually between four and six meters (roughly 13 to 19 feet) in length. As its name suggests, the diameter of the small intestine is smaller than the diameter of the large intestine, which makes up the last part of the GI tract. Food must be broken down into small molecules to be absorbed, and the small intestine is the place where most of that breakdown and absorption happens.

There are three regions of the small intestine. The first part is called the *duodenum*. This is the shortest part. It is about 25 centimeters (roughly 10 inches) long. The middle part of the small intestine is called the *jejunum*. The final part is the *ileum*. Together the jejunum and ileum are about 6 to 7 meters (roughly 19 to 22 feet) long. The ileum is the longest section of the small intestine, comprising about three-fifths of this amazing length. The distal end of the ileum connects to the colon (large intestine) at the *ileocecal junction*.

You are probably impressed to know that you have more than 19 feet of small intestine in your abdomen with room to spare. The small intestine's length is very important because most nutrient absorption takes place in the small intestine. The vast surface

area available along the length of the small intestine is required for nutrient uptake, but the organ's length is only the beginning of its story.

The small intestine is much more than a simple tube. Every feature is designed to make nutrient absorption an efficient process. Let's examine some of these, and then see how the three sections of the small intestine are further designed to capture all the nutrients possible, despite the changing characteristics of the material moving through it.

If you look into the small intestine's *lumen* (the inside of a tube), you will discover its surface is not smooth like that of a pipe or garden hose. Instead you will see lots of *circular folds* in the mucosa. LOTS of folds. These folds are about one centimeter (a little less than one-half inch) in height. The circular folds projecting into the lumen triple the surface area available for absorption.

Taking a closer look, you will find the surface of the circular folds is fuzzy. Their velvet-like texture is due to the presence of small finger-like or leaf-like projections called *villi*. The villi project into the lumen and are about 0.5 to 1.5 mm tall. The taller villi are in the duodenum and the shorter villi are in the ileum. In the center of each *villus* (singular of *villi*) is a tiny lymphatic vessel (called a *lacteal*) and a network of tiny capillaries. These small vessels transport nutrients absorbed from the intestinal lumen.

The circular folds triple the surface area of the small intestine, and the villi provide an additional ten-fold increase in the surface area available for nutrient absorption. But there's more.

On the surface of the villi are *microvilli*. Unlike villi, these are not projections of the whole mucosal lining. The microvilli are instead cell membrane-covered protrusions of the epithelial cells' cytoplasm. Each epithelial cell on the surface of a villus is equipped for absorption with about 3,000 microvilli! There are about 200 million microvilli in every square millimeter of the small intestine's

surface. They increase the surface area of the small intestine another twenty-fold.

The microvilli are also known as the *brush border*. In the brush border are enzymes that specifically aid in the break down and absorption of each kind of nutrient.

And thanks to all this folding, villi, and microvilli, the deceptively simple-looking small intestine has a mucosal surface area of about 250 square meters (2,700 square feet). That means you have inside your abdomen an absorptive surface area about the size of a tennis court!

But the small intestine's big surprises don't end with its phenomenal brush border. In its mucosal lining, in between the villi, are many pockets projecting down into the mucosa. These pockets are lined with epithelial cells equipped to secrete *intestinal juice,*

a watery substance that aids nutrient absorption. You recall that structures that secrete important substances are called glands. Therefore, these pockets are called *intestinal glands*. They are also called *crypts of Lieberkühn* after the 18th-century German anatomist who discovered them.

TAKING A CLOSER LOOK
Epithelial Cell with Microvilli

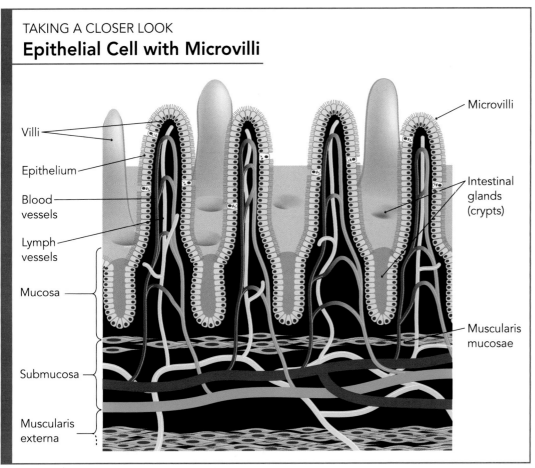

Interspersed among the epithelial cells covering the villi and lining the intestinal glands are several types of cells that perform very specific functions. *Goblet cells* — so named because they look like goblets under the microscope — produce the mucus that lubricates the surface of the lumen. *Paneth cells* in the crypts make special enzymes that kill certain undesirable bacteria. Not all bacteria in the GI tract are bad, as we will soon see. The Paneth cells help regulate the microbial population that lives inside you.

The majority of cells covering the small intestine's mucosa are *enterocytes*. These cells are the ones that have microvilli. Enterocytes are responsible for absorbing nutrients.

Additionally, deep in the wall of the small intestine are follicles of lymphoid tissue called *Peyer's patches*. This lymphoid tissue helps generate an immune response in the small intestine to keep harmful bacteria under control.

Before we finish this section, we must consider one more thing.

Remember our discussion of peristalsis in the esophagus? Well, peristalsis occurs in the small intestine, also.

Throughout the intestine, in the muscularis externa that surrounds the submucosa, are layers of smooth muscle. This smooth muscle is responsible for the coordinated contraction and relaxation of the small intestine. This coordinated activity propels

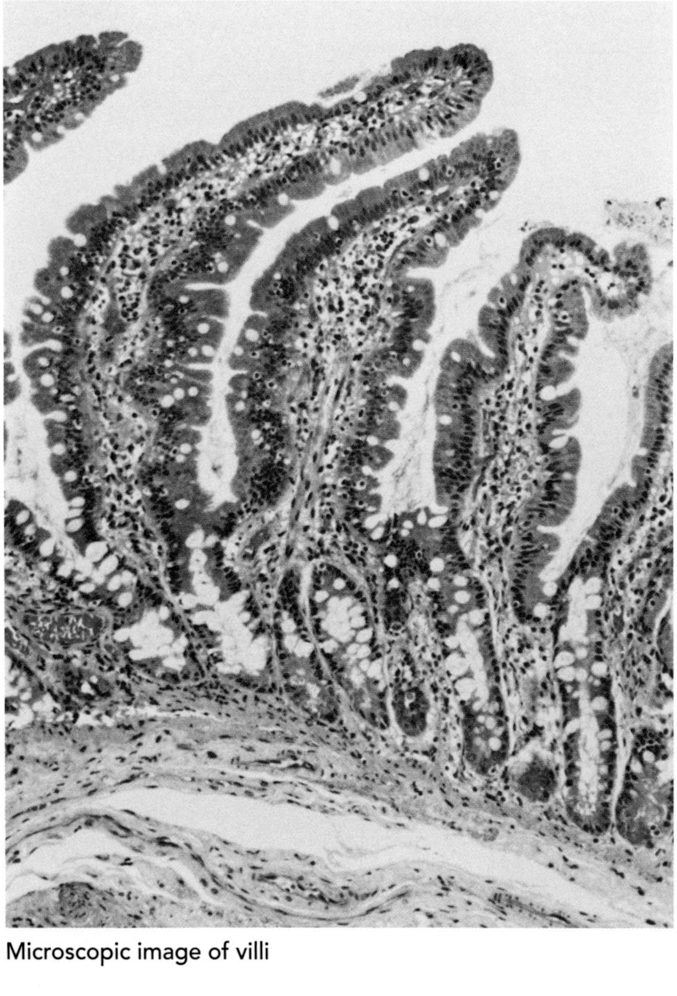

Microscopic image of villi

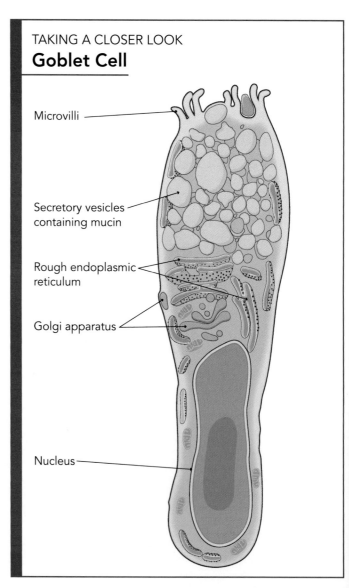

TAKING A CLOSER LOOK
Goblet Cell

Microvilli

Secretory vesicles containing mucin

Rough endoplasmic reticulum

Golgi apparatus

Nucleus

the contents of the GI tract along the length of the intestine. Again, this is peristalsis in action.

Also, consider the fact that smooth muscle is responsible for intestinal peristalsis. The peristaltic activity is involuntary and not under conscious control. It would be quite awkward if this were skeletal muscle under voluntary control. If you had to think about moving food along the small intestine, you would have to spend several hours a day just thinking about digesting your food.

And, as you may have already guessed, peristalsis occurs in the large intestine also.

How could anyone believe this amazing design happened all by accident? The vast organization of cells with specific functions all in the right places, arranged in a way to maximize absorptive surface area to just what human beings require. No, I can't either. . . .

Blood Supply of the Small Intestine

The duodenum gets arterial blood from two major arterial trunks that branch from the abdominal aorta, the same ones we learned about when discussing the pancreatic blood supply. These are the celiac trunk and the superior mesenteric artery. Blood reaches the duodenum from these two large arterial trunks through the *superior* and *inferior pancreaticoduodenal arteries,* respectively. Yes, that's really their names. But notice the names tell you which organs these arteries supply and whether they supply them from the top or the bottom.

Remember we said, when discussing the pancreas, that one branch of the celiac trunk supplies the body and tail of the pancreas with blood, and another branch of the celiac trunk supplies blood to the liver, stomach, duodenum, and head of the pancreas? Well, the superior pancreaticoduodenal artery comes from

that second branch. It brings blood to the duodenum and the head of the pancreas.

The duodenum and the head of the pancreas also receive arterial blood from the superior mesenteric artery, which branches from the aorta below the level of the celiac trunk. This blood reaches the duodenum and pancreas through the inferior pancreaticoduodenal artery. It is the very first branch of the superior mesenteric artery.

The arterial blood supply of the rest of the small intestine comes entirely from the superior mesenteric artery. Numerous jejunal and ileal branches carry blood toward the jejunum and ileum.

Because the jejunal and ileal arteries, 15 to 18 of them, run through the mesentery that enfolds the

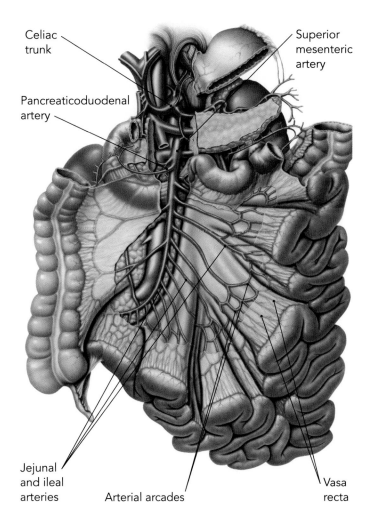

Celiac trunk

Superior mesenteric artery

Pancreaticoduodenal artery

Jejunal and ileal arteries

Arterial arcades

Vasa recta

Endoscopy

Some medical doctors specialize in the diagnosis and treatment of diseases of the digestive system. These doctors are called *gastroenterologists.* In evaluating patients, all sorts of techniques are used. The most important is the taking of a thorough medical history and performing a good physical examination of the patient. Other very important pieces of information can be obtained from blood tests, ultrasounds, X-rays, and computer tomography (CAT) scans.

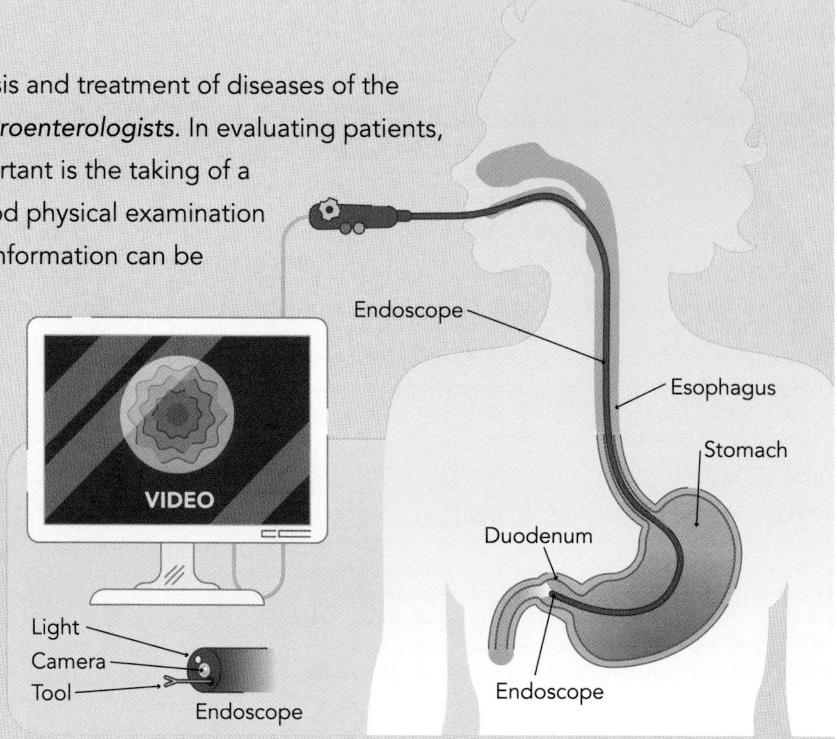

One of the most important diagnostic tools used by the gastroenterologist is the *endoscope.* An endoscope allows the doctor to look at the lining of the GI tract. Most endoscopes are flexible fiber optic devices. They have controls to allow the doctor to maneuver the scope as it is slowly advanced into the GI tract. Endoscopes have a light source for illumination. (After all, the doctor needs to see where he or she is going.) Most endoscopes even have a small channel through which the doctor can extend a pincer-like device that takes *biopsies* — samples of tissue for microscopic examination.

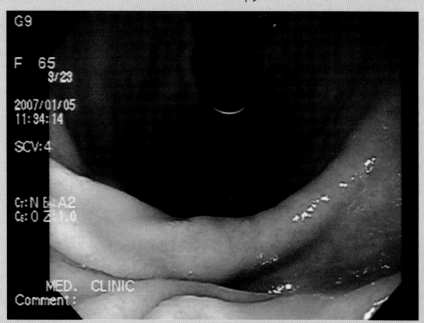

VIDEO

Endoscope

Esophagus

Stomach

Duodenum

Light
Camera
Tool

Endoscope

Endoscope

There are endoscopes suitable for evaluating both the upper and lower portions of the GI tract. Endoscopic examination of the upper GI tract (down to the level of the duodenum) is called **e**sophago**g**astro**d**uodenoscopy (yep, you heard it here first . . .), or EGD for short. Examination of the colon is called a colonoscopy.

Endoscopy is used to evaluate the stomach and duodenum to check for ulcers and inflammation. It can be used to discover the source of bleeding in either the upper or lower GI tract, to diagnose patients who have difficulty swallowing, and to remove foreign objects. Beyond a certain age, it is recommended that older adults undergo screening colonoscopy to screen for cancer of the colon.

Most endoscopic procedures can be done with only mild sedation. Usually the patient can go home an hour or so after the endoscopy is complete.

G9

F 65
3/23

2007/01/05
11:34:14

SCV:4

Cr:N E A2
Ce:0 Z 1.0

MED. CLINIC
Comment:

Endoscopic image of normal stomach in a healthy 65-year old woman. Permission of patient to publish this image was obtained.

small intestine, they do not get tangled trying to reach it, even though the 19 feet of small intestine is piled in a convoluted wad in the center of the abdomen. When these arteries get close to the small intestine, they merge into a series of arch-shaped *arterial arcades*. From these, many short straight arteries called *vasa recta* carry blood to each section along the entire length of the small intestine.

Venous drainage from the small intestine is primarily via the *superior mesenteric vein*. This vein drains into the portal vein, which takes blood to the liver.

Functions of the Small Intestine

Now that we've seen the structure of the small intestine, let's find out how it all works. Here goes . . .

As you recall, food enters the stomach and gets mixed with hydrochloric acid. This gets churned and mixed in the stomach. While still in the stomach, pepsin begins the process of breaking down proteins into smaller molecules that will be further broken down later. Partially digested food that is ready to leave the stomach is called *chyme*. Chyme is meted out of the stomach through the pyloric sphincter into the duodenum for further processing.

Being made up of partially digested food and hydrochloric acid, chyme is naturally very acidic. The enzymes that digest food in the duodenum are not designed to work in a highly acidic environment. And prolonged exposure to strong acid is not good for the lining of the small intestine. Therefore, in the duodenum, several things happen to neutralize this acid. First of all, the acid stimulates cells in the duodenum to secrete a hormone called *secretin* into the bloodstream. Secretin does two things. First, it signals the parietal cells in the stomach to lower their acid production. Second, the secretin triggers cells in the pancreas to make bicarbonate and

release it into the duodenum. This bicarbonate helps neutralize the acid.

Enzymes brought to the duodenum from the pancreas, particularly amylase, begin to break down starches in the chyme. Special enzymes along the brush border of the intestinal lining, each designed to break down a particular sort of nutrient, further metabolize sugars and starches. When adequately broken down, these nutrients are absorbed by the enterocytes and transported into the blood stream.

Other enzymes from the pancreas continue the breakdown of proteins into smaller and smaller units, ultimately into amino acids, the building blocks of proteins (more about that later). These amino acids are then absorbed.

When lipids are detected in the duodenum, another special hormone is secreted by the intestinal glands. This is called *cholecystokinin* (CCK). When CCK is secreted, it causes the gallbladder to contract. This contraction pushes some of the bile stored in the gallbladder into the duodenum. Here the bile helps break down lipids into smaller and smaller droplets. This process is called *emulsification*. Another enzyme from the pancreas, lipase, breaks down the lipid molecules into their smaller components. These are absorbed by the enterocytes covering the villi. Inside the enterocytes, the components of the lipid molecules are transformed into tiny packages suitable for transport. This involves reconstructing some of the lipid molecules that had to be broken down for absorption, and then enclosing the lipid molecules in carrier proteins. Fats are not water soluble and hence could not be safely carried in lymph fluid or blood. However, once enveloped by carrier proteins, they can be safely transported through a water-based fluid. These lipid transport packages — called *chylomicrons* — enter the lacteals, rather than the capillaries, in the center of the villi.

Ultimately, as nutrients are absorbed by the enterocytes in the small intestine, they are exported into the capillary beds and lacteals in the villi. The capillaries drain into ever larger venules and veins and then into the portal vein leading to the liver. In the liver, these nutrients are immediately available for processing. This, by the way, is part of the amazing design of the portal vein system. Most nutrients go directly to the liver without having to circulate throughout the body to reach their intended destination. And if any nutrients or absorbed chemicals are present in amounts that would not be good in the general circulation, the liver has a chance to process them before they cause harm. Lipids, having already been processed and packaged for safe transport in the cells lining the small intestine, are delivered directly into the bloodstream by the lymphatic system, which empties into a large vein near the heart.

The Large Intestine

The last organ in the GI tract is the large intestine, also called the *colon*. It has a larger diameter than the small intestine, but it is much shorter. The large intestine is only about 1.5 meters (5 feet) long.

The large intestine joins the small intestine at the *ileocecal junction*. This point of joining is also called the *ileocecal valve* because it prevents the backward movement of the intestinal contents into the small intestine. The most proximal portion of the large intestine is the pouch-like *cecum*. It is located in the right lower part of the abdomino-pelvic cavity. Protruding from the cecum, just beyond the ileocecal junction, is a small worm-shaped structure called the *appendix*.

TAKING A CLOSER LOOK
Large Intestine

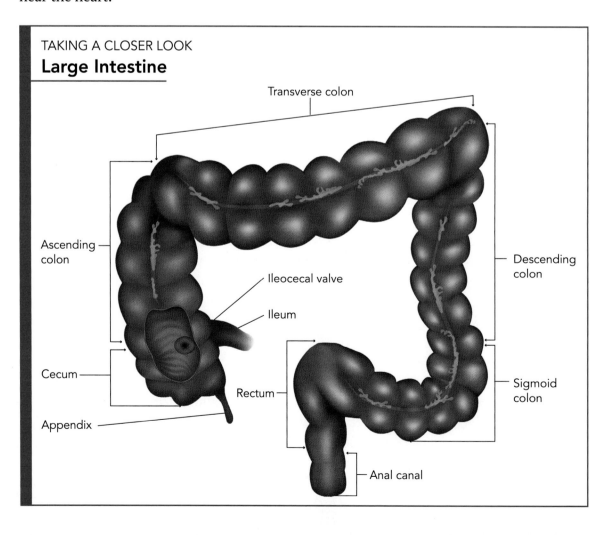

Transverse colon, Ascending colon, Ileocecal valve, Ileum, Cecum, Rectum, Appendix, Descending colon, Sigmoid colon, Anal canal

Moving up the right side of the abdominal cavity from the cecum, the large intestine is called the *ascending colon*. The colon then takes a sharp turn at the liver, and this bend is called the *hepatic flexure*. From the hepatic flexure, the *transverse colon* runs right to left across the upper part of the abdominal cavity. Then the colon turns sharply downward, and this sharp turn — because it is near the spleen — is called the *splenic flexure*. From there the colon, now called the *descending colon*, moves down the left side of the abdomen. On the lower left, it has an S-shaped region called the *sigmoid colon*. Finally, the sigmoid colon joins the *rectum* and then the *anal canal*. The *anal sphincter* marks the distal end of the colon.

If you were looking at the small and large intestines from a surgeon's point of view, you would notice several differences. The diameter of the large intestine is, of course, larger. Most of the small intestine is free to slide about, attached to its mesenteric membranes to protect it from twisting, but having a fair amount of free movement. The mesenteric attachments of the colon anchor it more firmly in place. Thus, the ascending colon is anchored to the right of the small intestine, the transverse colon runs superior to and slightly in front of the small intestine, the descending colon lies to the left, and the sigmoid colon is located inferior to the small intestine, which appears to be piled in the middle of the colon.

Diverticular Disease

In some people, examination of the colon will reveal small out-pouchings. These look like small sacs, not like the large sac-like haustra. These tiny outpouchings are areas where the colonic mucosa and submucosa protrude through weaknesses in the muscle layers. These small pouches are called *diverticula*. (Just one is called a *diverticulum*.) This condition is called *diverticulosis*. The majority of people with diverticulosis have no symptoms. Many are diagnosed during a routine screening colonoscopy, and if asymptomatic they require no special treatment. Other people may have some mild bleeding from the diverticula, but in the majority of these cases, this ceases without treatment.

However, diverticula can become infected. This is known as *diverticulitis*. Here, there is inflammation of the diverticula, and patients may have mild to moderate abdominal pain, nausea, and fever. Treatment for diverticulitis includes intravenous fluid and antibiotics. In the most severe cases, one or more diverticula may rupture. Then, infected material can leak into the abdominal cavity. In circumstances like these, surgery is sometimes necessary.

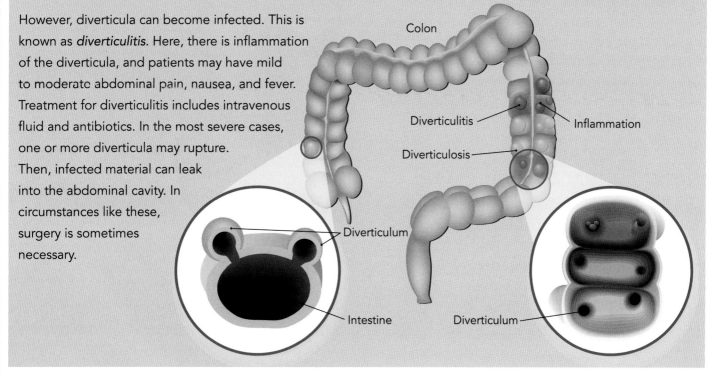

There are some other easily seen differences. There are three dense ribbon-like fibers running longitudinally along the colon from beginning to end. These are called *taenia coli*, which is Latin for "ribbons of the colon." These dense fibers pucker the colon into a series of large sacs called *haustra*.

If you were to compare the lumen of the small intestine to the lumen of the large intestine, you would note that the large intestine has no circular folds. There is some folding in the rectal mucosa, and none in the rest of the colon. There are also no villi in the large intestine. The reason for this design difference is obvious. The small intestine needs much more surface area because it is responsible for a much larger amount of absorption. Absorption does occur in the large intestine but on a much smaller scale. Mainly just water and electrolytes are absorbed in the colon. Therefore, the required surface area is far less.

Although there are no villi in the large intestine, the colon's mucosal cells do have microvilli. Also, there are intestinal glands in the large intestine. In these glands are many goblet cells which produce a lot of mucous. This mucous provides some lubrication for the passage of indigestible material along the colonic path toward the outside of the body. The mucous also protects the epithelial cells from being damaged by bacteria living in the large intestine.

Blood Supply of the Large Intestine

Arterial blood is delivered to the large intestine by branches of the *superior* and *inferior mesenteric arteries*. Venous drainage from the large intestine is via the *superior* and *inferior mesenteric veins*.

You may recall from the *Wonders Book* volume about the circulatory system that veins frequently follow roughly the same path as arteries and have similar names.

Functions of the Large Intestine

The large intestine has two primary functions.

First, it removes most of the water remaining in the material coming from the small intestine. The large intestine is very efficient. While the majority of absorption occurs in the small intestine, the large intestine absorbs about 80 percent of the water remaining in the material that enters it.

Second, the large intestine processes any remaining indigestible material into its final form called *feces* (or stool). Feces is then stored in the rectum until it is eliminated.

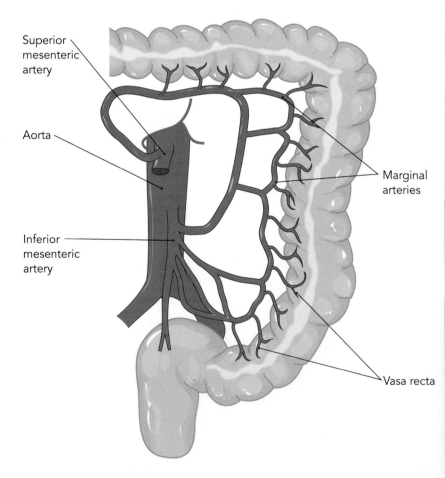

Superior mesenteric artery

Aorta

Inferior mesenteric artery

Marginal arteries

Vasa recta

Appendicitis

Appendicitis is inflammation of the appendix. This can occur when the lumen of the appendix is blocked, perhaps by feces or by inflammation from a viral infection. The appendix has a small lumen, and if it cannot drain properly, bacteria get trapped in it. Inflammation and infection then follow and can result in damage to the tissue in and around the appendix.

The symptoms of appendicitis typically include fever, nausea, elevated white blood cell count, and tenderness in the right lower quadrant of the abdomen. Because appendicitis is often associated with inflammation of the nearby peritoneal lining of the abdomen, sudden movement of the abdominal wall usually causes severe pain in the right lower quadrant.

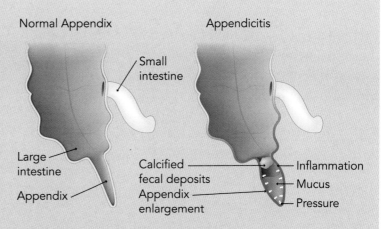

The most common treatment is surgery to remove the appendix. Surgeons usually proceed to surgery quickly when appendicitis is suspected. This is because the risk of complications is high if the appendix ruptures.

Is the Appendix a Vestigial Organ?

Have you ever heard the term "vestigial organ"? It refers to a part of the human body that has supposedly lost or changed its function during our evolutionary journey from ape-like creatures to modern humans. Remember, I said "supposedly. . . ."

Over the last 150 years, many structures in the body were said to be leftovers from our evolutionary past. They were said to be "leftover" structures because they were thought to have no active function and to serve no purpose in our bodies. The coccyx (tip of the sacrum), the pineal gland, the thymus gland, wisdom teeth, ear muscles, and tonsils are just a few "vestigial" body structures that have been touted as evidence for evolution. Scientists who think, or thought, this were wrong about all of these. We now realize that these "vestigial" organs are not useless but have very real functions in the body. So much for those evidences of evolution.

Perhaps more than any other organ, the appendix has been called a vestigial organ. Many have suggested that the appendix is left over from our evolutionary past when our diets were higher in fiber, and we had a much larger cecum. That belief paints a picture of a cecum shrinking over millions of years to leave only the appendix. That is an interesting story, but it's just not true.

It turns out that the appendix does have a function after all. It helps maintain the balance of bacteria in the colon. Furthermore, the lymphoid tissue in the appendix plays a role in the immune system. You can get along without your appendix, but that doesn't mean it is useless or that it is a vestige — a footprint — of an evolutionary past.

Our Creator did not put any useless organs in our bodies. Some structures serve an important function only in a developing baby. Some serve functions in a mature person. But just because you don't know what something does, does not mean it has no function. Sometimes you just need to look harder.

Bacteria in the Intestines

Bacteria are bad, right? After all, people spend lots of time and energy trying to kill bacteria (germs) or at least avoid contact with them. Bacteria cause disease and harm people.

Fortunately, that's not always the case. There are lots of circumstances where bacteria provide great benefits. This is especially true when it comes to the digestive system.

Many people are surprised to learn that our digestive system houses many, many different types of bacteria. Some estimates suggest that there may be somewhere between 800 and 1,000 varieties of bacteria in the GI tract. These bacteria reside primarily in the large intestine, with fewer living in the stomach and small intestine.

Flatulence

Belching is gas expelled from the upper GI tract. But we know that gas can be expelled from the lower GI tract also. This is known as flatulence. Practically everyone has experienced this at one time or another.

Actually, passing gas from the rectum is a normal bodily function. The amount and frequency of flatus varies from person to person.

Whereas belching is most often the result of swallowing air, flatulence is most often the result of gases produced in the lower GI tract itself. This gas production is the result of bacteria fermenting undigested sugars and starches that enter the large intestine. On average, between 500 and 800 ml of bowel gas is produced daily.

Of the total bowel gas produced each day, approximately 99 percent is odor-free. This portion consists mainly of oxygen, nitrogen, carbon dioxide, and methane. The remaining 1 percent gives bowel gas its unpleasant smell. This portion is composed of gases such as hydrogen sulfide and methyl mercaptan, among others.

The daily amount of flatus is increased with the indigestion of certain foods containing large amounts of certain complex carbohydrates. These foods include beans, dairy products, turnips, and sweet potatoes.

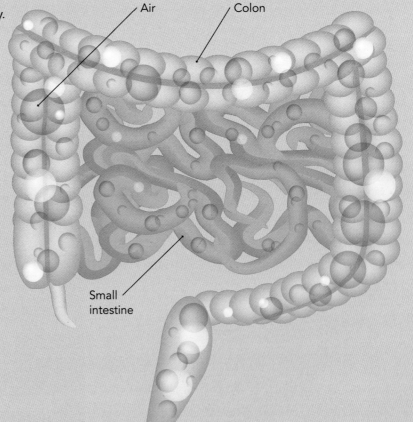

Air

Colon

Small intestine

The number of bacteria in the large intestine is enormous. Between 50 and 60 percent of our feces solids is made up of bacteria.

Bacteria that normally live in or on our bodies, often helping us in some way, are called our *microbiome.* Intestinal bacteria are an important part of the human microbiome.

Antibiotic-Induced Diarrhea

As we have seen, the bacteria in the GI tract can benefit the body in many ways. One of the most important is where the presence of "good" bacteria protects the body from "bad" bacteria. Nowhere is this more evident than in hospitals.

Hospitals are obviously full of sick people. Sick people often needs lots of antibiotics. This can be a very good thing, as antibiotics save many lives and relieve much suffering. But there is a price to be paid for the blessing of antibiotics.

You see, antibiotics kill bacteria. That's their purpose. Unfortunately, the antibiotics administered to kill the bacteria infecting a patient also kill lots of the "good" bacteria in the intestine. When this happens, *antibiotic-induced diarrhea* can develop. The population of "good" bacteria is drastically decreased, and many "bad" diarrhea-causing bacteria take the opportunity to grow unchecked. One of the most common "bad" bacteria is called *Clostridium difficile.* It can cause *pseudomembranous colitis*, an illness characterized by severe inflammation of the large intestine.

Although some cases of antibiotic-induced diarrhea are relatively mild and respond quickly to treatment, some severe cases can lead to death. Pseudomembranous colitis can be quite difficult to treat. Over the years, strains of *Clostridium difficile* that are resistant to antibiotics have become more prevalent in bacterial populations, so cases of pseudomembranous colitis are more and more challenging to cure.

There are many beneficial functions served by these bacteria. First, the presence of so many *non-pathogenic bacteria* (bacteria that do not cause disease) can prevent more harmful bacteria from becoming a problem. This is because the "good" bacteria use lots of the energy resources in the intestine. This leaves a very small nutrient supply for the "bad" bacteria. Usually, the good bacteria out-compete the bad bacteria for resources, thus keeping the bad ones in check.

Next, many bacteria in the large intestine help process some of the undigested material as it passes through. This bacterial processing can break down material in a way that our normal digestive processes cannot. These bacteria can, in effect, recover nutrients that would otherwise be lost.

Also, some bacteria manufacture certain very important substances. Biotin (vitamin B7), which is needed for proper cell growth and the production of fatty acids, is produced by intestinal bacteria. Folate (folic acid) helps prevent anemia and is important during pregnancy to prevent some birth defects. This is also produced by bacteria in the digestive system. One of the most important products of our internal bacteria is vitamin K. This vitamin is important in the production of special proteins called clotting factors. These clotting factors are needed for blood to clot.

"Good" bacteria are "good" when they live where they are supposed to live. That is, in the lumen of the GI tract. If these "good" bacteria found their way into the blood stream, they could then become very "bad." That is why lymphoid tissues and other immune system functions are active in the walls of the GI tract. These protective mechanisms help keep our bodies safe from accidental invasion by the "good" bacteria.

4

NUTRITION AND METABOLISM

God designed the digestive system to break down and absorb all the different sorts of nutrients in our food and drink. Now we need to see what happens to each of these after absorption. What happens to all those nutrients after they enter the blood stream? And what happens to the indigestible fiber in our food? It also serves a purpose.

Let's find out. . . .

Classes of Nutrients

There are many different nutrients in the food we eat. These are then broken down into an even more confusing collection of smaller substances, all with long, multisyllabic names. How can we make sense of all this?

Actually, it is pretty simple if you begin at the beginning and take it one step at a time. First of all, we need a definition. A *nutrient* is a substance in food that is used by the body to live and grow. Nutrients from food become the fuel and chemical building blocks of the body. Without a proper supply of nutrients, the body could not make or store energy. It could not repair damaged tissues or build new tissue. The body could not grow.

Most often, nutrients are divided into six classes, or categories. You certainly have heard of all these at one time or another. Nutrient classes include: carbohydrates, proteins, lipids, water, vitamins, and minerals. These classes can be further divided into two main divisions, macronutrients and micronutrients. (*Macro-* means "large" and *micro-* means "small." Perhaps you can guess where this is going.)

Macronutrients are the types of nutrients that the body needs in large amounts. These are the nutrients needed for production of energy and the building of tissues. Fortunately, the bulk of our diet is made up of macronutrients. These are carbohydrates, protein, and lipids.

Micronutrients, on the other hand, are also substances needed by the body, but in much smaller amounts. This does not mean they are not important for body functions, quite the opposite. Micronutrients are vitamins and minerals. These nutrients participate

Read Before Proceeding!

Before going any farther, please take a deep breath.

We are about to embark on a journey through the different classes of nutrients. You will find it truly fascinating.

However (yeah, there's that "however" again . . .), to help you best understand this material, it is necessary to show you a number of chemical diagrams. DO NOT let all these structures intimidate you. No one expects you to remember these complex structures or understand every detail about them . . . at least for now. In medical school, students learn a bazillion of these things, but that is still a few years away. By then, you will understand much of the information these diagrams summarize and may, like many of us, find them quite enjoyable. Admittedly, the love of chemical diagrams is a bit of an acquired taste.

For now, you just need to get a general idea about how the different sorts of molecules are put together. You will be able to see where and how the carbon, oxygen, hydrogen, and sometimes, nitrogen atoms are put together. The diagrams illustrate that and reveal the patterns that make nutritional knowledge easier to understand.

Relax, and just get the big picture for now.

in, and help regulate, many body functions.

For our study, we will consider the final nutrient, water, all on its own.

Last but not least, there is one more definition. An *essential nutrient* is something the body either cannot make on its own or cannot make fast enough to meet the body's needs. Thus, these nutrients must be obtained from the diet. Examples of these would be certain amino acids (called, not surprisingly, "essential" amino acids), certain fatty acids, and some vitamins. We will cover essential nutrients as we explore the nutrient classes in more detail.

How carbohydrates, proteins, and lipids are broken down.

Carbohydrates	Proteins	Lipids (fats)
↓	↓	↓
Enzymes	Enzymes	Enzymes
↓	↓	↓
Glucose	Amino acids	Fatty acids and glycerol

Carbohydrates

Carbohydrates are what we commonly call sugars and starches. Their primary use in the body is as a source of energy. The quick energy boost a candy bar gives you when you are hiking comes from the sugar in the candy bar.

Carbohydrate molecules are made up of three kinds of atoms. These are carbon (C) atoms, hydrogen (H) atoms, and oxygen (O) atoms. The way these atoms

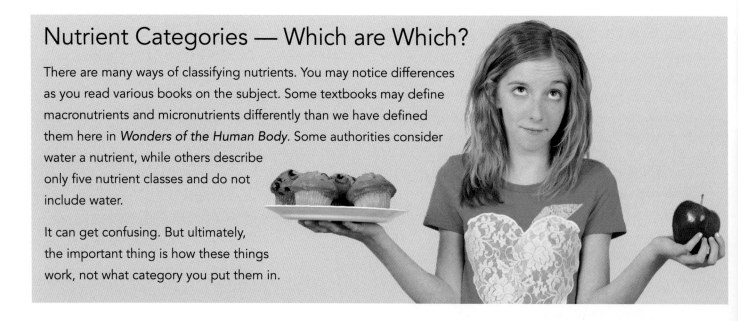

Nutrient Categories — Which are Which?

There are many ways of classifying nutrients. You may notice differences as you read various books on the subject. Some textbooks may define macronutrients and micronutrients differently than we have defined them here in *Wonders of the Human Body*. Some authorities consider water a nutrient, while others describe only five nutrient classes and do not include water.

It can get confusing. But ultimately, the important thing is how these things work, not what category you put them in.

are arranged is what defines a carbohydrate and what gives it the properties it has.

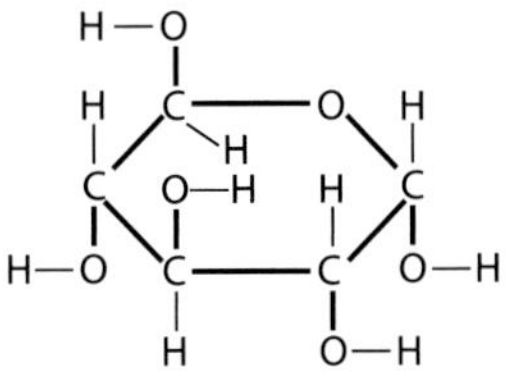

There are two major types of carbohydrates: *simple carbohydrates* and *complex carbohydrates*. Simple carbohydrates are sugars. Sugars — simple carbohydrates — consist of single molecular units containing only 6 or 12 carbons each, along with the appropriate number of oxygens and hydrogens. By linking these smaller units together, much larger and more complex carbohydrates — such as starches — can be produced.

A carbohydrate consisting of a single six-carbon sugar molecule is called a *monosaccharide*. Glucose, galactose, and fructose are good examples of monosaccharides ("mono" meaning one, "saccharide" meaning sugar). Glucose is the favorite fuel of living cells, especially those in the brain. Fructose is commonly called "fruit sugar" because it is plentiful in fruits. Honey contains both fructose and glucose.

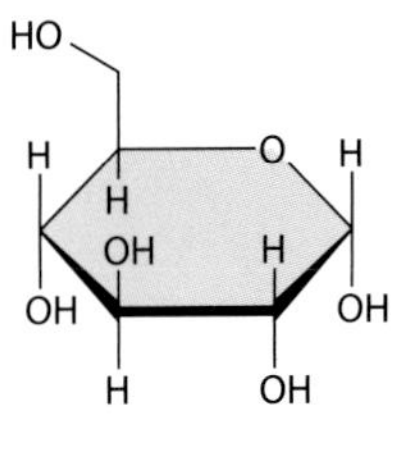

Glucose 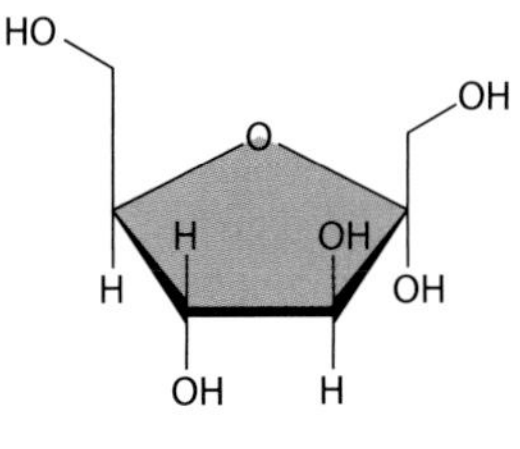 *Fructose* 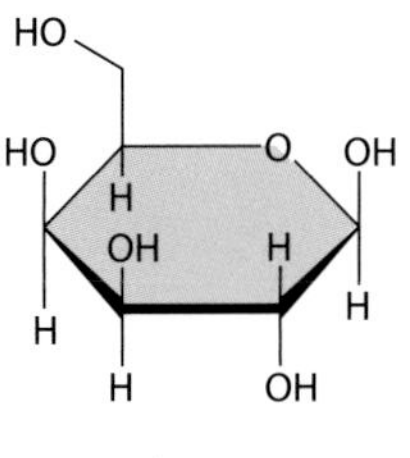 *Galactose*

A carbohydrate made of two six-carbon sugar molecules linked together is a *disaccharide*. A very familiar disaccharide is sucrose. Sucrose is ordinary table sugar. This disaccharide is made by linking together one molecule of glucose and one molecule of the sugar fructose. Other disaccharides include maltose (made of two molecules of glucose) and lactose (made of one molecule of glucose and one molecule of galactose). Lactose is the sugar found in milk.

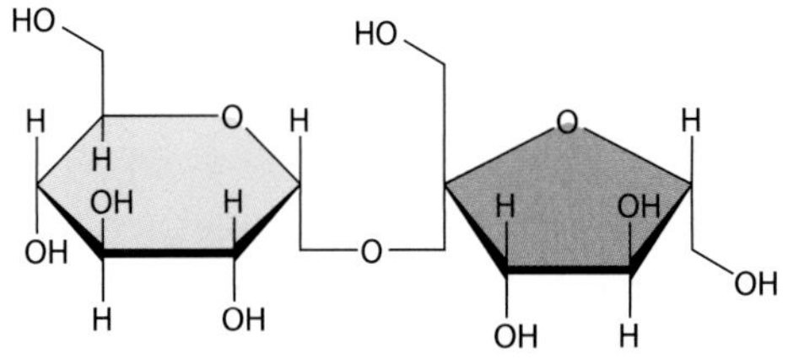

Sucrose

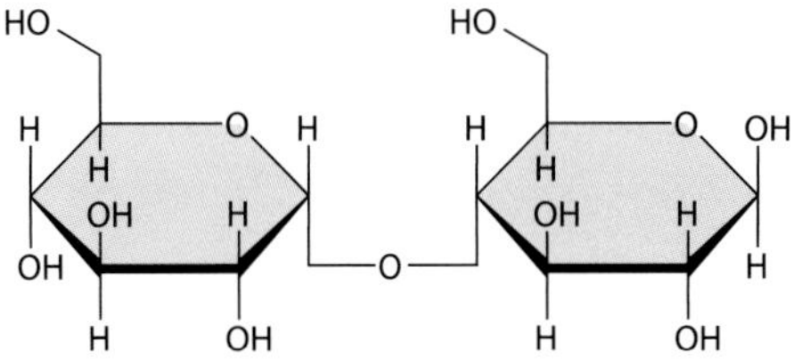

Maltose

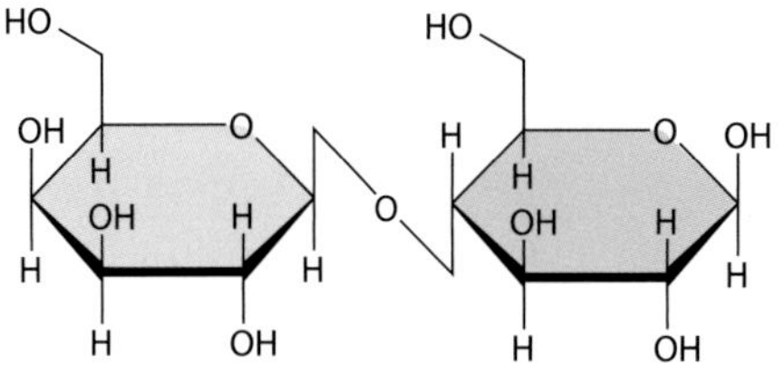

Lactose

Complex carbohydrates are, as you might have guessed, made up of much larger numbers of saccharide units. Complex carbohydrates are therefore called *polysaccharides*. *Poly* means "many," and polysaccharides can contain a huge number of saccharide units. Moreover, as the structures get bigger, their shapes can get more complicated. For example, some polysaccharides are long straight chains of sugar subunits. Other polysaccharides have a structure that is branched. These structural differences as well as the way the saccharide subunits are attached to each other give polysaccharides widely differing properties.

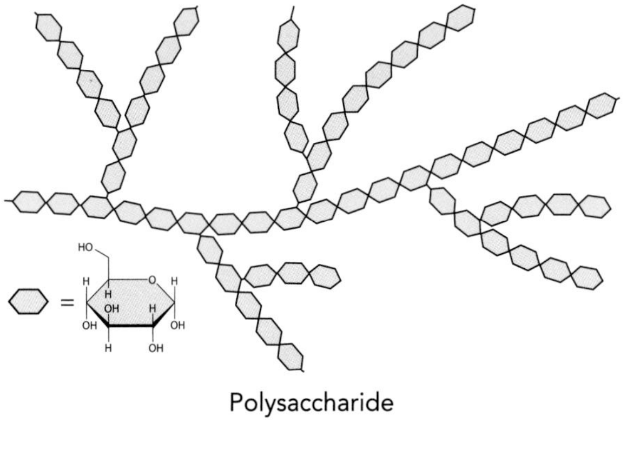

Polysaccharide

A primary function of polysaccharides is for the storage of energy. *Starches* are a good example of this. Starch is a polysaccharide made up of many, many glucose molecules linked together. Starch is made by plants. It is found in potatoes, rice, and wheat. When starch is digested, the bonds holding the glucose molecules together are broken. The long chain ultimately becomes lots and lots of single glucose molecules. Remember, we said that glucose is the living cell's favorite fuel. Therefore, starch is an excellent source of energy.

Another important polysaccharide is *glycogen*. Like starch, glycogen molecules are also polymers of glucose, but they are more branched than starch. Glycogen is sometimes called "animal starch" because animals and people store most of their glucose in the form of glycogen. Glycogen, like starch, is easily broken down into its glucose components and is therefore a good source of readily accessible energy.

When glucose is abundant — like after you eat — the liver and skeletal muscles convert glucose into glycogen. The glycogen is stored in the liver and in muscle. Later, when more energy is required, the glycogen in the liver is broken down to supply glucose for the whole body.

Muscles utilize their stores of glycogen exclusively for themselves, making it possible to move quickly without waiting on fuel to arrive from the liver. Muscles deplete their glycogen during heavy exercise but are designed to rapidly rebuild it from the glucose available in the bloodstream. Muscles respond to the demands of training by building up and increasing the amount of glycogen they store.

Polysaccharides are not just used to provide energy. Some polysaccharides cannot be digested by the human body. An example is cellulose, which is a primary component of the cell wall in plants. We call cellulose a *structural carbohydrate*. The glucose molecules comprising cellulose are attached to each other in a way that cannot be broken by the enzymes in our bodies. While not useful as a source of energy, cellulose provides much of the fiber in our diet. Dietary fiber affects the movement — or *motility* — of the material in our digestive tract as well as the efficiency of some digestive processes.

TAKING A CLOSER LOOK
Disaccharides and Monosaccharides

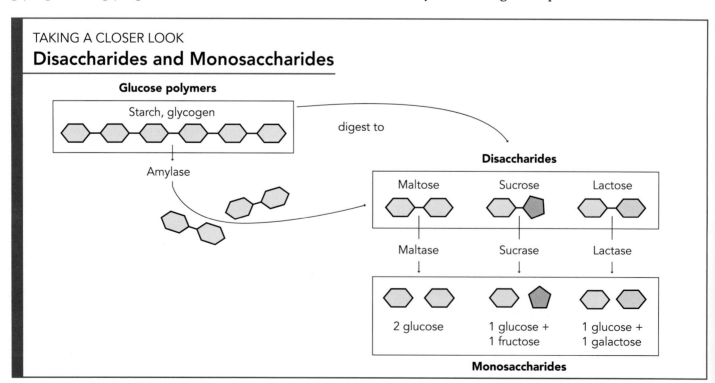

Digestion of Carbohydrates

Lots of carbohydrates are found in the typical diet. Many people consume a diet far too high in carbohydrates. Simple sugars come from fruit, honey, and milk, as well as the sugars in candy and ice cream. More complex carbohydrates enter the body via the starches in rice, wheat, crackers, and vegetables.

The digestion of carbohydrates begins while you are chewing, when salivary amylase starts breaking some of the glucose-to-glucose bonds in starch. However, carbohydrate digestion really takes off when chyme from the stomach enters the duodenum.

There, under the action of pancreatic amylase, starches are aggressively broken into smaller and smaller saccharide units. Then, at the brush borders of the microvilli, these saccharide units are finally converted into monosaccharides by the action of specific enzymes, each designed to break the links between particular monosaccharides. These include enzymes such as sucrase and lactase. As you might guess, sucrase separates the glucose-fructose bond found in sucrose, and lactase separates the glucose-galactose bond found in lactose.

The enterocytes in the small intestine can only absorb monosaccharides. Therefore, the digestive process must be complete in order for transport into

Lactose Intolerance

Do you know anyone who says they cannot drink milk? People with lactose intolerance cannot fully digest and absorb the lactose in the milk and other dairy products they consume. This is not dangerous, but the diarrhea, gassiness, and bloating it causes is inconvenient and uncomfortable.

Human babies, like the babies of mammalian animals, are normally born able to digest milk. Lactose, the disaccharide sugar in milk, must be broken down into its simpler components — glucose and galactose — in the small intestine in order to be absorbed. Lactase, the enzyme that breaks down lactose, is produced by cells lining the small intestine. In premature babies, activation of the gene coding for lactase is sometimes delayed. And in much of the world's population, this gene is downregulated after weaning, eventually producing varying degrees of lactose intolerance.

Adults whose genes are not downregulated are said to have "lactase persistence." However, even lactose-intolerant people have the genetic information coding for lactase enzyme; it is just switched off. Whether or not the lactase gene remains active in adulthood is determined by a person's genes. Certain geographic populations, like people descended from northern European or Middle Eastern peoples — have a higher prevalence of lactose tolerance — or "lactase persistence" — than others.

the blood stream to take place. After absorption by the enterocytes, monosaccharides diffuse into capillaries in the villi and are taken via the portal circulation to the liver.

Proteins

Proteins are the building blocks of all living things. The primary structural component of all the body's tissues — muscle, tendons, ligaments, hair, skin, teeth, the various organs, and even bone — are proteins. The enzymes that regulate the many chemical reactions in the body are proteins. Antibodies — molecules produced by the immune system — are proteins. Many of the hormones used by the body to signal other parts of the body are proteins. A good example is insulin, which controls the level of glucose in the blood and is a protein hormone. The clotting factors that keep you from bleeding to death from cuts are proteins. Yes, proteins are very important. Three-quarters of your dry body weight consists of protein!

Proteins are molecules that are made of carbon (C), nitrogen (N), oxygen (O), and hydrogen (H). Given that they are so important and that they serve so many different functions in the body, it is obvious that proteins exist in an enormous variety of forms. They are certainly the most complex of the macronutrients.

TAKING A CLOSER LOOK
Proteins

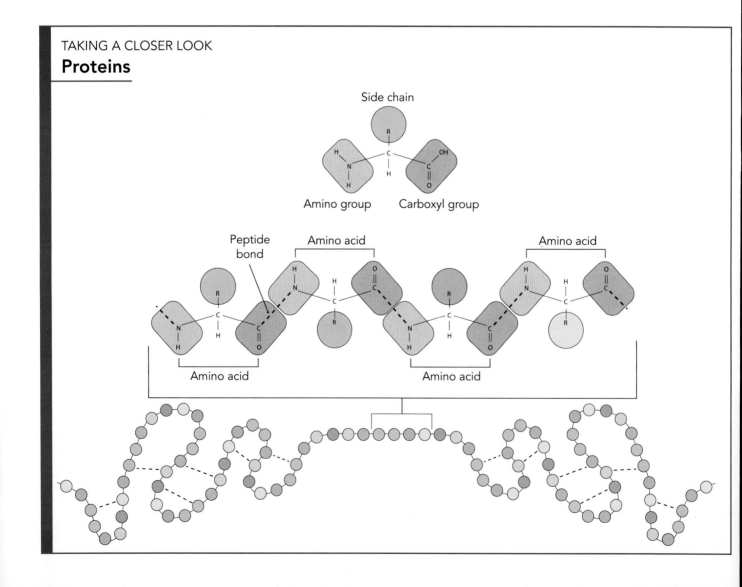

In carbohydrates, the building block is a sugar molecule, or monosaccharide. The basic building blocks of proteins are called *amino acids*. About 500 different amino acids exist, but there are only 20 different amino acids in the human body. Just as more complex carbohydrates are made by linking more and more monosaccharides together, linking more and more amino acids together produces larger and larger proteins.

Amino acids are linked together by a *peptide bond*. Two amino acids linked together are called a *dipeptide*. Three linked amino acids are a *tripeptide*. The number of amino acids linked together can be in the thousands. Generally speaking, a chain of 50 or fewer amino acids is called a *peptide*. A chain longer than 50 amino acids is called a *protein*.

When you stop to think about it, there is an overwhelming number of possible combination of amino acids. Let's demonstrate by building a simple peptide.

If a peptide were only one amino acid long, how many possibilities would be possible? Yep, 20 is the right answer, assuming we are only talking about peptides in the human body. If our peptide were two amino acids long, how many possibilities would we have? Yep, 20 choices for the first one and 20 choices for the second one. So how many different combinations do we have for a two-amino acid peptide? Well, 20 times 20 equal 400! As you see already, this can get to be a very big number very quickly.

If we wanted to build a six-amino acid peptide, how many possible combinations would there be? Well, six positions with 20 possible amino acids at each position means 20 times 20 times 20 times 20 times 20 times 20! That is 64,000,000 possible combinations! And even with these enormous numbers of possibilities for molecules containing a particular number of amino acids, it happens that

the number of possibilities is even larger when we learn that the same collection of amino acids can be arranged in different ways. Each of those variations has different characteristics. For instance, many bio-active molecules exist in two mirror image forms, a "right handed" form and a "left handed" form. Only one of the two mirror image forms "works" in the body, the other being useless.

This enormous number of possible combinations helps us understand the incredible variety among proteins. It is little wonder why God designed the human body, and all living things, using so many of them. And because we need to live in the world with other living things, sharing the same resources and even consuming the proteins contained in them — whether soybeans, wheat bread, or hamburgers — it is easy to see why God used many of the same sorts of proteins in humans, animals, and other living things. If He had not, the proteins and other nutrients we eat would not be compatible with our body's enzymes. We need protein nutrients from our diet to grow, to replace worn out or damaged cells, and to make the many protein chemicals vital to cellular function and daily life.

Essential and Non-Essential Amino Acids

Fortunately, the body is able to manufacture certain amino acids even if they are not consumed in adequate amounts. These are called *non-essential* amino acids. They are not non-essential because they are unimportant but because you can make them from scratch. If the body needs one of these and there are none available in the diet, the body simply takes other materials and synthesizes that amino acid.

Now the unfortunate part. Some amino acids cannot be synthesized by the body. These amino acids must be provided by dietary intake. These are called *essential amino acids*, and there are nine of them in adults. (Nine amino acids are essential for babies and children. Debate continues among

experts as to whether eight or all nine are essential in the adult diet.)

We do not have to have all the essentials at every meal, but a balanced diet should ideally provide them every day. Fortunately, all unprocessed foods contain the essential amino acids we need, so they are not difficult to include in your diet unless you live on processed junk foods.

If we do not obtain all the essential amino acids from our diet, the proteins requiring them cannot be made without demolishing other proteins — such as those in muscles — and recycling their amino acids. Our

AMINO ACID	MOLECULAR STRUCTURE	ESSENTIAL/ NON-ESSENTIAL
Alanine		Non-essential
Arginine		Non-essential
Asparagine		Non-essential
Aspartic acid		Non-essential
Cysteine		Non-essential
Glutamine		Non-essential
Glutamic acid		Non-essential
Glycine		Non-essential
Histidine		Essential
Isoleucine		Essential

AMINO ACID	MOLECULAR STRUCTURE	ESSENTIAL/ NON-ESSENTIAL
Leucine		Essential
Lysine		Essential
Methionine		Essential
Phenylalanine		Essential
Proline		Non-essential
Serine		Non-essential
Threonine		Essential
Tryptophan		Essential
Tyrosine		Non-essential
Valine		Essential

fitness and health can suffer. Interestingly, the amino acids "essential" for humans do not necessarily match those essential for various other living things.

Digestion of Proteins

In the digestion of carbohydrates, larger polysaccharides must be reduced to their simplest monosaccharide components in order to be absorbed and utilized by the body. The same can be said of proteins. Their long peptide chains are broken down into their amino acid components during the process of digestion.

Saliva has no real effect on protein, so protein digestion begins in the stomach. Once in the stomach, **pep**sin (the activated form of the proenzyme pepsinogen) begins to break **pep**tide bonds in the long amino acids chains. Shorter chains called *polypeptides* are the result.

When chyme passes into the duodenum, more *proteases* (protein-digesting enzymes) act on proteins. These pancreatic proteases include trypsin, chymotrypsin, and carboxypeptidase. Further and further the long chains of amino acids are broken down. Then the very small peptide fragments remaining encounter more than a dozen additional

proteases on the brush border of the microvilli. The end result is a mixture of extremely short peptides and single amino acids. While a fair number of dipeptides and tripeptides — peptides just two or three amino acids long — are absorbed by the enterocytes, most of these are broken down into single amino acids by the time they are released into the capillaries and sent to the liver.

Once amino acids reach the liver via the portal circulation, they enter a busy biological factory. Depending on the body's needs, the amino acids absorbed from the diet may have many possible fates.

Amino acids from the diet can be used as the raw material to synthesize other non-essential amino acids. That way, so long as the diet contains all the essential amino acids, there will be enough of all the amino acids to make proteins.

Remember, though, that amino acids are the building blocks of proteins. Therefore, not surprisingly, the liver uses amino acids from the food you eat to build a lot of new protein molecules. One of these, albumin, is the main protein found in blood plasma. The liver also makes all the proteins required to make your blood clot properly, as well as the proteins necessary to break up blood clots once they've served their purpose. The long list of proteins made in the liver includes many proteins designed to carry minerals and other molecules safely through the blood.

Amino acids not used to build proteins or make other amino acids can be turned into glucose or even lipids by the liver, but first the nitrogen atoms in them must be removed. You recall that proteins all contain nitrogen atoms, in addition to the carbon, hydrogen, and oxygen atoms found in carbohydrates and lipids.

The nitrogen atoms in proteins are part of little subunits called "amine groups." That's how amino acids got their name. Every amino acid contains at least one amine group. Well, in the liver, amino acids can be converted to glucose or lipids after first removing the nitrogen-containing amines from the molecules.

Do Intact Proteins Ever Get Absorbed?

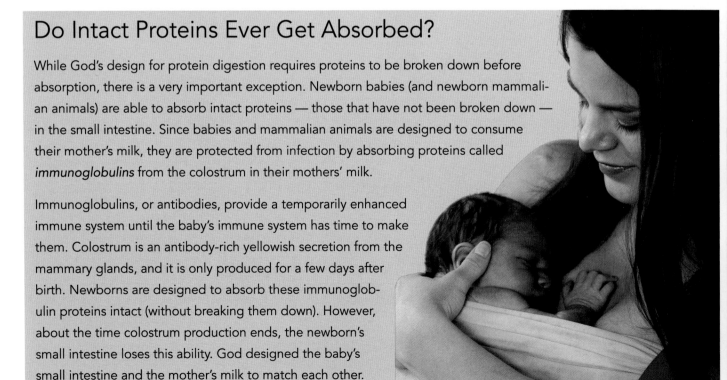

While God's design for protein digestion requires proteins to be broken down before absorption, there is a very important exception. Newborn babies (and newborn mammalian animals) are able to absorb intact proteins — those that have not been broken down — in the small intestine. Since babies and mammalian animals are designed to consume their mother's milk, they are protected from infection by absorbing proteins called *immunoglobulins* from the colostrum in their mothers' milk.

Immunoglobulins, or antibodies, provide a temporarily enhanced immune system until the baby's immune system has time to make them. Colostrum is an antibody-rich yellowish secretion from the mammary glands, and it is only produced for a few days after birth. Newborns are designed to absorb these immunoglobulin proteins intact (without breaking them down). However, about the time colostrum production ends, the newborn's small intestine loses this ability. God designed the baby's small intestine and the mother's milk to match each other.

Once nitrogen is removed from amino acids, it must be disposed of. The first step in this process produces a toxic waste product, ammonia. Not to fear, however. The liver converts ammonia to a small organic molecule called urea. Urea can be safely transported in the blood to the kidneys, where it is excreted in the urine.

Lipids

Lipids are a somewhat more complicated group of substances. Like carbohydrates, they are made of carbon (C), oxygen (O), and hydrogen (H). However, these atoms are found in different proportions in lipids than in carbohydrates. Some lipids — the phospholipids — also have nitrogen and phosphorus atoms, too. A major difference between lipids and carbohydrates is that lipids are not soluble in water, whereas many simpler carbohydrates are.

The difference in water solubility and other properties of lipids and carbohydrates is due largely to the way that atoms are arranged and to the fact that there are proportionately a lot more carbon-hydrogen bonds in lipids than in carbohydrates. Organic molecules with more oxygen atoms in them tend to be water soluble, but long chains of carbon and hydrogen atoms are more likely to float on top of water.

Lipids include several types of compounds including fatty acids, triglycerides, phospholipids, and steroids. The term *fat* is often used as a synonym for *lipid,* although this is not strictly accurate in every situation, and usage varies. In the kitchen, fats are solid at room temperature and oils are liquid, and the term *lipid* is virtually unheard of. (Ever hear of your mom melting "a tablespoon of lipid" in the pan? Or "trimming the lipid" off the steaks?) In human anatomy, we never refer to the "layer of lipid" under the skin or the globules of lipid stored in the omentum. But we do refer to the lipid layer called the myelin sheath that covers our nerves. In discussing nutrition, *fats* and *lipids* are often used interchangeably.

In the chemistry lab, *fat* generally refers to triglycerides, a particular kind of lipid. In fact, triglycerides are the storage form of lipid the body makes when we eat more calories than we burn. Butter, lard, bacon fat, coconut oil, olive oil, peanut oil, and all vegetable oils are also triglycerides.

A *triglyceride* molecule consists of one molecule of glycerol attached to three fatty acid chains. In the name, *tri-* means "three" and *–glyceride* refers to the glycerol backbone. Glycerol is not a fat but is instead a water-soluble, three-carbon molecule that forms the backbone of a triglyceride molecule. *Fatty acids* are chains of carbon and hydrogen atoms with just

TAKING A CLOSER LOOK
Triglyceride Molecules

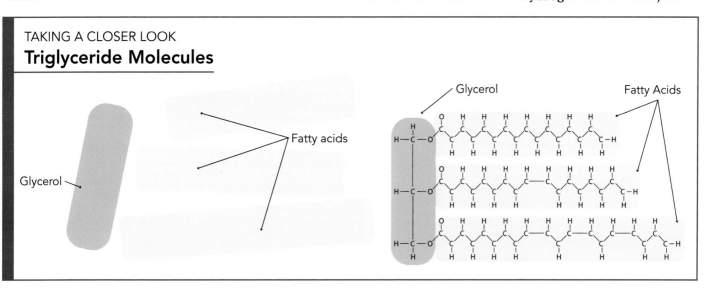

a couple of oxygen atoms on one end. They are the simplest lipid. Three fatty acid chains are attached to glycerol to make a triglyceride molecule.

Fatty acid chains with lots and lots of hydrogen atoms are called *saturated* and tend to be found in triglycerides that are solid at room temperature. Fatty acid chains with proportionately fewer hydrogen atoms are called *unsaturated* and tend to be found in oils.

When triglycerides are broken down, their glycerol components can be transformed into glucose sugar. The fatty acid chains can be metabolized as a fuel source. When we eat more calories than we need, the extra energy can be stored in the bonds of fatty acid chains. More than twice the energy can be stored

High Cholesterol

Cholesterol is important to the proper function of the human body. It is vital to cell membrane structure. Cholesterol plays a key role in the synthesis of steroid hormones. We need cholesterol.

So why is everybody so down on cholesterol? The simple answer is that, yes, we do need it. We just don't need too much.

Over the years, doctors have seen a relationship between high cholesterol and heart disease. People with higher than normal cholesterol levels have a higher than normal risk of heart disease.

Normal artery

Sometimes a small blockage (or even several) begins to develop in a person's coronary arteries. Cholesterol is a key component of these blockages. As the blockage (often called a *plaque*) grows, the blood flow to the heart muscle is decreased. This can worsen until the heart itself cannot get enough oxygen to function adequately. Often, the result is a heart attack. This same process can also affect the blood vessels supplying the brain, leading to a stroke.

Beginning of plaque formation

Cholesterol is transported in the blood by means of proteins called lipoproteins. There are two primary types of the proteins, low-density lipoprotein (LDL) and high-density lipoprotein (HDL). LDL is often called "bad" cholesterol and HDL is called "good" cholesterol. This is because high levels of LDL are strongly associated with an increased risk of heart disease and stroke. HDL, on the other hand, can reduce the risk of heart disease. HDL takes excessive amounts of LDL to the liver to be processed and recycled. HDL also helps keep the walls of the heart's arteries clean and healthy.

Fatty deposit accumulation

Patients are routinely screened for high levels of LDL. This is particularly true for people with additional risk factors, such as a strong family history of heart disease, smoking, high blood pressure, or diabetes.

In a person with high LDL, the goal is obviously to lower it. The primary method of treatment is controlling the diet and increasing activity. When diet and exercise do not adequately lower the LDL, then there are medications that can be used. Sometimes a combination of medications must be used to get an adequate result.

Narrowed artery blocked by a blood clot

In any case, a serious effort should be made to reduce LDL. Lowering LDL has been shown to lower the risk for heart disease and stroke.

in fat than in the same amount of carbohydrate or protein. Therefore, triglycerides provide an efficient form of energy storage, a material that is easily broken down when extra energy is needed.

Phospholipids resemble triglycerides. They are built on a glycerol backbone, but contain just two fatty acid chains. In the third spot on the glycerol backbone, a different subunit is attached, one containing phosphorus, nitrogen, and oxygen atoms. Due to the arrangement of atoms in a phospholipid, part of the molecule is soluble in water and part is not. (The water-soluble *phosphor-* end is called *hydrophilic,* or "water-loving," and the water-insoluble *-lipid* end is called *hydrophobic,* or "water-fearing.")

Phospholipids are perfect as the key structural component of all cell membranes. Cell membranes consist of a double layer of phospholipids. These phospholipids are arranged so that their hydrophilic ends face the inside and outside of the cell. Their hydrophobic fatty acid tails point to the inside of this "phospholipid sandwich." This is a very stable arrangement in which other important molecules are anchored to make the cell membrane an effective barrier and controller of what can enter a cell.

Steroids are the last type of lipid to be considered here. These are large, complex molecules that do not look anything like triglycerides or fatty acids. They are made of four carbon rings with varying side chains. The most important lipid for our study here is actually called a *sterol*. This is, of course, *cholesterol*.

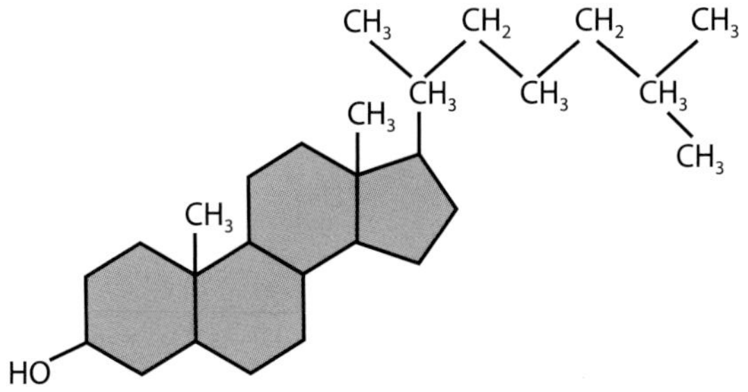

Cholesterol chemical structure

Cholesterol has gotten a bad reputation because of the association of "high cholesterol" with heart disease, but you cannot live without cholesterol. Cholesterol is a vital component of cell membranes, making them more flexible and fluid than they would be if they were only made of a phospholipid sandwich. Further, cholesterol is the starting raw material for the synthesis of the steroid hormones in the body. You may have heard of testosterone and estrogen, for instance. They are made from cholesterol. Cholesterol is transported in the blood attached to specific transport proteins called *lipoproteins*. There are several types of lipoproteins, but the two most common are low-density lipoprotein (LDL) and high-density lipoprotein (HDL).

TAKING A CLOSER LOOK

Phospholipids

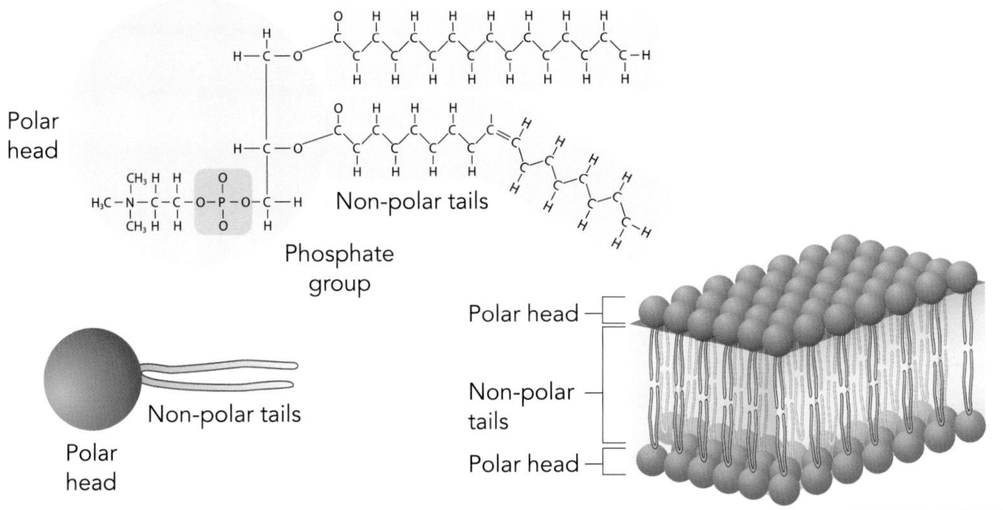

Digestion of Lipids

As mentioned previously, lipids are not soluble in water. At first glance, this might seem to be a bit of a problem. After all, the fluids throughout the digestive tract are primarily water. And if oil and water do not mix, how do you digest lipids?

As it turns out, there's no problem at all. Our Master Designer has this taken care of.

When lipids are ingested, they are introduced to a watery environment. Because they are not soluble in water, the lipid particles gather together to form droplets, or globules. In this form, the lipid-digesting enzymes (*lipases*) do not have adequate access to the molecules inside the droplet. Little digestion can take place in this manner.

However, also in the duodenum are found bile salts. Remember, these are a component of the bile produced by the liver and stored in the gallbladder. The bile salts break up these larger droplets into smaller and smaller droplets. This process is called *emulsification*. Since there are now many, many more smaller droplets there is a much greater surface area on which the lipases can act. The lipids are broken down.

The next issue is that these breakdown products of lipid digestion are also not soluble in water. Again, no problem. The bile salts then associate with these much smaller breakdown products to form *micelles*. Micelles are tiny collections of lipid digestive products. These are so small that they are able, even in this watery environment, to find their way to the enterocytes where absorption takes place.

Once inside the enterocyte, some processing of the lipids takes place. Before leaving the cell, lipid components recently liberated by lipases for absorption are used to re-make triglycerides. These triglycerides are combined with lipoproteins to form *chylomicrons*. Chylomicrons are water-soluble droplets that are taken outside the enterocyte via exocytosis. Once outside the cell, chylomicrons leave the villi in the *lacteals* — the lymphatic vessels in the center of each villus — and are ultimately emptied into the venous system.

Vitamins

You always hear about vitamins. Take your vitamins. Vitamins are good for you. You have probably taken some type of vitamin supplement, perhaps chewables shaped like your favorite cartoon characters. But do you know what vitamins are? You will soon.

Vitamins are the first of two groups of micronutrients we will consider. As you recall, micronutrients are important for proper function of the body, but only in small amounts. Since small amounts are sufficient, it seems obvious that they are not useful sources of energy, like carbohydrates, which are required in much larger amounts.

Vitamins assist the body in processing and utilizing other nutrients. Also, to be a vitamin, the substance cannot be produced by the body, or at least not produced in adequate amounts. Most vitamins come from the diet, and some (vitamin K especially, and some of the B vitamins) are produced by *gut flora* — the "good" bacteria living in the intestines.

There are 13 vitamins, and they are divided into two groups: *fat-soluble* and *water-soluble*.

The fat-soluble vitamins bind to lipids during digestion and are absorbed along with them. These are vitamin A, vitamin, D, vitamin E, and vitamin K. These vitamins can be stored by the body.

The remaining vitamins are water-soluble. This means that they do not need the presence of lipids to aid in absorption. On the other hand, it also means that these vitamins are not stored in the body. Excesses of these vitamins are simply removed from the body in the urine.

Vitamin Deficiencies

Since the body cannot make vitamins, or at least enough of them, there is always a risk that we might develop a vitamin deficiency if we do not consume enough of them. A vitamin deficiency can result from an inadequate diet or from the inability to absorb the vitamin from food.

Because vitamins are needed by so many different processes in the body, but only in small amounts, and because most vitamins are found in a wide variety of foods, it took scientists a long time to discover their importance. Just think, before medical scientists had a way to know which foods had which vitamins, or to decipher the many things that could go wrong in the case of a severe deficiency, diagnosing and treating deficiency diseases was largely a matter of trial and error and guesswork. Long sea voyages proved to be the cause of a very specific vitamin deficiency, however, and one of the easiest to treat.

Scurvy Makes History

Scurvy, the result of severe vitamin C deficiency, was once a leading cause of death among the crews of ships on long voyages. During the age of exploration, beginning in the late 15th century, seamen from many countries discovered that the preventative and cure for scurvy was the regular consumption of citrus fruit.

British sailors acquired the nickname "Limeys" because the British Royal Navy in 1799 began requiring their seamen to drink lemon juice during long stints at sea to prevent scurvy. Scottish surgeon James Lind had shown in 1753 that citrus fruit could prevent scurvy, but it took time for the idea to catch on. After that, British sailors could stay at sea for two full years without developing the dreaded disease that had once killed so many.

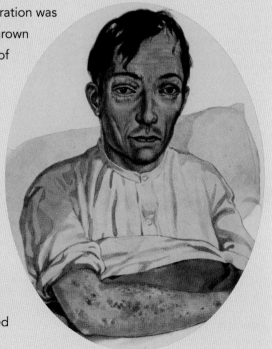

Lemons were imported by the navy from continental Europe. The citrus ration was eventually switched from lemon juice to lime juice because limes were grown in British colonies. Sadly, no one knew that lime juice contained far less of the mysterious yet-to-be-identified scurvy-preventative than lemons. To make matters worse, the lime juice was stored for long periods of time, leading to degradation of the vitamin C in it. Scurvy reappeared. This temporarily discredited the value of citrus fruit to prevent scurvy.

It was a long time before vitamin C itself was identified and definitively linked to scurvy. Most mammals possess the enzyme required to make vitamin C for themselves and therefore do not get scurvy. That made studying the disease tricky. Finally, in the 20th century, scientists studying *beriberi* — a disease caused by a deficiency of *thiamine* (vitamin B1) — accidentally found that guinea pigs on a grain-only diet got scurvy instead of beriberi. In 1932, scientists discovered the vitamin C molecule, also called *ascorbic acid*, and were able to show it prevented scurvy in guinea pigs and in people.

In years past, sailors on long sea voyages often developed a disease called *scurvy,* due to the prolonged and complete lack of fresh fruits and vegetables in their diet. Scurvy is a vitamin C deficiency. Sailors suffering from scurvy developed weakness, muscle soreness, bleeding gums, and their teeth often fell out. Many died.

Vitamin C is important for the proper synthesis of collagen, the main structural protein in connective tissue. Because vitamin C is a water-soluble vitamin, our bodies cannot store it. After a month or so without any vitamin C, the body cannot repair and maintain its collagen-dependent tissues — cartilage, bones, tendons, ligaments, blood vessels, skin, gums, intestines, the dentin in teeth, and so many more. Scurvy gets worse the longer a person is deprived of vitamin C, and it caused many aboard long sea voyages to weaken and die. Because vitamin C is present in many fresh fruits and vegetables, and because just a small amount is sufficient to prevent scurvy, it took a long time to be certain that scurvy was directly related to a vitamin deficiency.

Vitamin A is needed to make light-sensitive pigments in the retina. Of course, vitamin A, like all the vitamins, has many functions in many different tissues. Because the light-absorbing molecule

VITAMIN	SOLUBILITY	DEFICIENCY DISEASE	FOOD SOURCES
Vitamin A	Fat	Night blindness, hyperkeratosis, and keratomalacia	Liver, orange, ripe yellow fruits, leafy vegetables, carrots, pumpkin, squash, spinach, fish, soy milk, milk
Vitamin B1 (Thiamine)	Water	Beriberi, Wernicke-Korsakoff syndrome	Pork, oatmeal, brown rice, vegetables, potatoes, liver, eggs
Vitamin B2 (Riboflavin)	Water	Glossitis, angular stomatitis	Dairy products, bananas, popcorn, green beans, asparagus
Vitamin B3 (Niacin)	Water	Pellagra	Meat, fish, eggs, many vegetables, mushrooms, tree nuts
Vitamin B5	Water	Paresthesia	Meat, broccoli, avocados
Vitamin B6	Water	Anemia, peripheral neuropathy	Meat, vegetables, tree nuts, bananas
Vitamin B7 (Biotin)	Water	Dermatitis, enteritis	Raw egg yolk, liver, peanuts, leafy green vegetables
Vitamin B9 (Folate)	Water	Megaloblastic anemia, deficiency during pregnancy is associated with birth defects, such as neural tube defects	Leafy vegetables, pasta, bread, cereal, liver
Vitamin B12	Water	Pernicious anemia	Meat, poultry, fish, eggs, milk
Vitamin C (Ascorbic acid)	Water	Scurvy	Many fruits and vegetables, liver
Vitamin D	Fat	Rickets and osteomalacia	Fish, eggs, liver, mushrooms
Vitamin E	Fat	Deficiency is very rare	Many fruits and vegetables, nuts and seeds
Vitamin K	Fat	Bleeding diathesis	Leafy green vegetables such as spinach, egg yolks, liver

required to see in low light is rapidly used up and must be regenerated, the first vitamin A deficiency symptom to appear is night blindness.

Because fat soluble vitamins are stored, it is possible to overdose on them. While it would be unusual to do so while eating an ordinary balanced diet, it is possible to consume toxic amounts. The classic example of this is vitamin A. The vitamin A concentration in polar bear liver is so huge that explorers trapped in the Arctic long ago reported getting sick after eating a lot of it. Unless you eat an awful lot of liver and fish, however, you probably get most of your vitamin A from orange, yellow, and green fruits and vegetables, like carrots. You cannot overdose on the vitamin A obtained from plant sources because they do not contain vitamin A itself

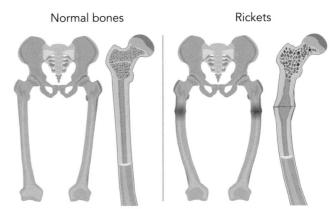

Normal bones   Rickets

Rickets can result from prolonged vitamin D and calcium deficiencies.

but only a precursor — carotene — from which your body makes the vitamin A it needs.

You see that there are a lot of vitamin B's, and chemically they are all very different. They each have distinctly different roles in cellular metabolism. The eight water-soluble B vitamins are all used in the chemical reactions that obtain energy from nutrients. B vitamins also participate in the process of making red blood cells. Most of the B vitamins also have other common names. Vitamin B1 is thiamine. Vitamin B2 is riboflavin. And vitamin B3 is niacin. Vitamin B7 is biotin, and almost everyone just calls it biotin. Vitamin B9 is folic acid, and folic acid is the name it goes by, too. Vitamin B6 and vitamin B12 generally go by their letter-number names.

The B vitamins are found in many foods, including meat and fish, eggs and dairy, beans and peas, whole grains and leafy green vegetables. While chemically different, they all tend to be found together in the same foods. All the B vitamins are present in whole grain, but some are missing from processed grains. Beriberi, a thiamine deficiency, became more common in Asia after processing rice became popular. Processed wheat flour, from which the wheat germ is removed to enhance shelf life, is also missing some of the B vitamins found in the whole wheat products. For this reason, bread made commercially from processed wheat flour is now generally "enriched" by the addition of some of the B vitamins.

Why Are Vitamins Named With Letters?

The first vitamin to be discovered was vitamin A. Being the first, it was creatively called "fat-soluble A." The next to be discovered was therefore given the equally imaginative name, "water-soluble B." But then another B vitamin, riboflavin, was discovered. Riboflavin was designated "vitamin B2" and the first B vitamin became vitamin B1. All seemed simple until scientists discovered that vitamin B1 was really two separate vitamins. The B2 name was already taken, so these were named B1, or thiamine, and vitamin B3, or niacin. Later, scientists discovered and named more B vitamins, but some of these turned out not to be B vitamins at all, and their numbers were retired.

Meanwhile, the precedent of naming vitamins with letters was established. Vitamin D was so named because it was the fourth sort of vitamin to be discovered. Likewise, for vitamin E. Vitamin K, essential for the synthesis of clotting factors, was named for the German word for coagulation, *Koagulationsvitamin*.

A deficiency of vitamin B6 or vitamin B12 can cause anemia. Vitamin B12 deficiency can result from either a lack of B12 in the diet (poor intake) or a lack of intrinsic factor. Remember, intrinsic factor is produced by the parietal cells in the stomach, and it is required for vitamin B12 to be absorbed in the small intestine. Vitamin B12 deficiency can cause pernicious anemia with its associated neurological symptoms like a sore tongue and numb feet.

Vitamin D aids in absorption of calcium from the GI tract and in the utilization of calcium as it fulfills its many roles in bones and other tissues. Calcium is required to build and maintain strong bones. Prolonged vitamin D deficiency, with the calcium deficiency that accompanies it, can lead to *rickets* in children and *osteomalacia* in adults. Children with rickets have poorly mineralized bones that may hurt, deform as they grow, and fracture easily. Adults with osteomalacia — "thin bones" — also suffer from bowing of the legs and back and are very susceptible to bone fractures.

Vitamin D is called "the sunshine vitamin." It is produced by a chemical reaction in our skin when exposed to sunlight. For some people, this might be enough vitamin D, but not for everyone. Vitamin D

is abundant in fish oils, and is also found in liver, cheese, and egg yolk, but the diet of many people used to provide insufficient vitamin D. This made rickets a common problem until it became a popular practice to fortify milk with vitamin D. Whether produced in the skin or absorbed from food and milk, vitamin D must be activated in the liver or kidney before it goes to work helping calcium remodel and strengthen bones.

Vitamin E is an *antioxidant.* Many of its functions are related to its ability to destroy unstable chemical by-products called "free radicals" before they can oxidize and destroy cell membranes. This is especially important in the brain, where damaged nerve cells cannot be replaced. Vitamin E molecules embed themselves in cell membranes and destroy any free radicals that come close. Because LDL-cholesterol becomes a more dangerous artery-clogging substance when oxidized, vitamin E's ability to remove free radicals also helps protect the heart. Vitamin E's functions go beyond its antioxidant work. It also decreases the tendency for platelets to aggregate into sticky artery-clogging plaque.

Vitamin K is required for the synthesis of many *coagulation factors* — proteins that make it possible for blood to clot. A lack of vitamin K can then obviously lead to a tendency to bruise or bleed easily. Large amounts of Vitamin K are produced by bacteria living in the intestine. Vitamin K is also abundant in dark green leafy vegetables.

You can see that vitamins are small but vital — *vital* substances you need in minuscule amounts. Yet God, who designed our bodies to require these substances, placed all the micronutrients we need in the foods we eat or provided additional sources for them, like our gut flora and the sunshine-fueled processes in our skin. Your best bet for nutritional health is to eat a balanced diet consisting mostly of foods that have not been processed so much that the nutrients we need have been removed.

Minerals

Minerals are another class of micronutrients. These are inorganic substances that, like vitamins, are not used for energy. They are, however, quite important for the proper functioning of the body. Even though we only need minerals in a small amount each day, they surprisingly make up about 5 percent of the body mass of an average person.

Calcium and phosphorus account for the majority of the mineral content of the body. This is not surprising because they are very important components of the bones in our body. And we have lots of bones!

However, other minerals present in far smaller amounts are equally important.

Iron is a part of hemoglobin. Hemoglobin molecules, packed into red blood cells, carry oxygen all through your body. Insufficient iron levels cause low hemoglobin and iron-deficiency anemia. People with anemia often suffer from fatigue and shortness of breath. Iron-rich foods include red meat, pork, poultry, seafood, beans, peas, raisins, and spinach. Vitamin C-containing foods, eaten at the same time as iron-rich foods, help your body absorb iron.

Fluoride helps increase the mineral density of teeth and bones. How much this benefits bones is still debated. However, fluoride definitely helps remineralize the enamel covering teeth, restoring minerals lost from exposure to acids in the mouth and decreasing the risk of tooth decay. Fluoride is added to most toothpastes and many public water supplies. But fluoride also occurs naturally in many foods. Tea contains quite a bit of fluoride. It is also found in raisins, carrots, potatoes, and seafood.

Copper must be consumed in small quantities as it is a necessary component of many enzymes. These enzymes are required for the proper function of cells and tissues throughout the body. So that you don't absorb too much or too little copper, your body regulates how much copper is absorbed from your food and how much is gotten rid of through the body's excretory processes. Copper is found in a wide range of foods from both animal and plant sources, so if you eat a balanced diet, you should get all you need.

Iodine is necessary for the production of thyroid hormone. This hormone helps regulate the body's metabolic rate. People suffering from an iodine deficiency may develop a *goiter* — an enlargement of the thyroid gland due to its attempts to make enough hormone despite the lack of sufficient iodine. Iodine deficiency during pregnancy can cause mental retardation in babies.

Iodine is found in many foods, such as seafood, eggs, yogurt, milk, and cheese. Nevertheless, iodine deficiency was once a big problem in many regions of the United States and Canada until the introduction of iodized salt. Unfortunately, iodine deficiency continues to afflict much of the world's population.

In our modern diet, these minerals are all readily available. However, as is always the case, a balanced diet is the best defense against a vitamin or mineral deficiency.

Water

Water is essential to life. It is as simple as that. Depending on conditions (temperature, humidity, etc.) and activity level, many people would die without water after three or four days. Few would survive beyond seven to ten days. After all, at least half of the body is water. In men, water makes up 55–60 percent of the body. In women, the percentage is slightly less at around 50–55 percent.

Adequate water intake is needed to maintain enough blood volume to ensure adequate blood pressure and

MINERAL	FUNCTIONS	DIETARY SOURCES	SYMPTOMS OF DEFICIENCY
Calcium	Needed for formation of teeth and bones. Important for proper function of muscle and nerves, blood clotting.	Dairy products, greens, legumes	Poor growth, loss of bone (osteoporosis)
Chlorine	Important in the formation of stomach acid (HCL) and in maintaining acid-base balance	Table salt (sodium chloride)	Muscle cramps
Chromium	Needed for proper metabolism of lipids and carbohydrates	Liver, seafood, some vegetables	Abnormal glucose metabolism
Copper	Needed for electron transport in energy production, a cofactor in iron metabolism	Nuts, legumes, seafood	Anemia, peripheral neuropathy
Iodine	Vital in production of thyroid hormones	Grains, iodized salt	Enlarged thyroid (goiter)
Iron	Required for hemoglobin production	Meats, green leafy vegetables, whole grains	Iron deficiency anemia
Magnesium	Required for function of nerve and muscle tissue	Green leafy vegetables, legumes, nuts	Muscle cramps, weakness, loss of appetite
Manganese	An important cofactor in many enzyme reactions	Vegetables, fruits	Abnormal bone formation, poor wound healing
Molybdenum	An important cofactor in many enzyme reactions	Grains, legumes	Seizures, intellectual disability
Phosphorus	Important in the formation of teeth and bones, aids in maintaining acid-base balance	Meats, dairy products	Weakness, calcium loss
Potassium	Needed for proper function of nerves and muscles	Fruits and vegetables, grains	Weakness, muscle cramps, abnormal cardiac rhythms
Selenium	Antioxidant, needed for proper immune system function	Whole grains, meats, seafood	Abnormal thyroid hormone function, myocardial necrosis
Sodium	Helps maintain proper fluid balance, important in blood pressure control	Table salt	Weakness, confusion, loss of appetite
Zinc	Component of many enzymes	Grains, meat, seafood	Skin abnormalities, impaired immune function

circulation. Water is lost in the process of removing wastes from the body via urine and cooling the body through the evaporation of sweat. You even lose water in every breath you exhale. These losses must be replaced. You get the idea.

In the digestive system, water is a vital component. It is a part of saliva, as well as a major portion of the gastric fluids and intestinal juice secreted in the GI tract. The majority of the water secreted into the GI tract is reabsorbed in the small and large intestines. Only a very small amount of water is lost in the feces.

How much water should you drink each day? Popular wisdom says to drink eight 8-ounce glasses of water each day. That's not a bad idea, but in truth, the amount of water each person needs varies a lot. You might need more or less, depending on your weight, health, and activity level. Certainly, you need more when you exercise, sweat, have a fever, or suffer from a gastrointestinal upset.

It is particularly important to stay hydrated before, during, and after exercise. And it is vital to hydrate yourself *even before you feel thirsty* when it is hot or when you are actively sweating. For instance, occupational health experts recommend moderately active people in moderate conditions should drink at least a cup of water every 15 to 20 minutes. The harder the work and the hotter the conditions, the

more hydration is needed. Good hydration is the best way to prevent dangerous heat illnesses like heat stroke, situations in which the body's ability to cool itself can fail, leading to a dangerous elevation of body temperature.

Fiber

Recall our discussion of the polysaccharide *cellulose*. Cellulose is the main structural protein in plants. We take in cellulose when we eat fruits and vegetables.

Unlike other types of polysaccharides, cellulose is not broken down by our digestive system and used for energy. Quite the opposite. Cellulose is essentially indigestible by humans. However, cellulose is an important part of our diet because it a major source of fiber.

There are additional plant parts that qualify as fiber. *Dietary fiber* includes all the edible parts of plants that we cannot digest. Some of the dietary fiber, like cellulose, is insoluble in water. Insoluble fiber does not absorb water, and it moves through our GI tract virtually unchanged. Most insoluble fiber comes from the bran layer of grain. Such fiber makes the movement of material through the intestines more efficient. Fiber aids in the formation of feces by producing a bulky mass on which peristalsis can act, making the elimination of solid waste material more efficient.

Some dietary fiber is soluble in water. Soluble fiber comes from fruits and vegetables, peas and beans, and cereal grains like barley, oats, and oatmeal. Soluble fiber absorbs water and swells to form a gel-like material. This material also increases the bulk of the material moving through the intestines. In addition, it makes the absorption of sugars more gradual and can decrease the absorption of cholesterol.

So be sure to get your fiber daily!

How much water is in your body?

Adult male	Adult female	Children	Infant
60%	55%	65%	75%

Our Dietary Needs

It seems like everybody talks about diets. There always seems to be some new fad diet being discussed. People should eat more of this and less of that. More protein. Less protein. More carbohydrates. More fat. Less fat. More meat. Less meat. Where does it end?

Well, frankly it is not the purpose of *Wonders of the Human Body* to recommend any particular type of diet. It is a difficult task to give specific recommendations because there are many things to be considered. Do you need to lose weight? Do you need to gain weight? How active are you? Are you

training to meet any athletic goals? Do you have any special medical conditions? Are you a rapidly growing teenager? All these things, and more, need to be taken into consideration when determining a person's proper diet.

It is best to consider some general guidelines and leave it at that.

Let's first talk calories. A calorie is a unit of energy. The calorie used in chemical laboratories is the amount of energy needed to raise the temperature of one gram of water one degree Celsius at one atmosphere of pressure. A food calorie is 1,000 times that much energy. Of course, food calories are used to provide the energy to keep the cells in your body functioning, not to heat water in a laboratory. From here on, the calories we refer to will be food calories.

The amount of energy a person needs to obtain from food each day varies. On average, a man needs around 2,400 food calories each day. A woman needs about 1,800. The difference is largely due to the difference in the size and muscle mass that typically distinguishes even the fittest men and women. A man and woman of the same size, at rest, will not burn the same amount of energy. The man will burn about 20 percent more. Why? Because muscle forms a larger percentage of his body mass than the woman's. Muscle tissue has a higher metabolic rate than body fat.

The carbohydrates, proteins, and fats we eat can all be turned into energy, and much of it is. The amount of energy that can be obtained by metabolizing all the macronutrients a

Estimated Calorie Needs Per Day to Maintain Your Current Weight:

To just meet your BMR (Basal Metabolic Rate) = HBW (Healthy Body Weight) x 10

To meet your BMR and:

• A sedentary lifestyle (i.e., you sit all day) = HBW x 13

• Light activity (i.e., you walk around campus) = HBW x 15

• Moderate activity
  (i.e., you exercise 60 min. 4-5 times per week) = HBW x 17

• Heavy activity (i.e., you are an athlete) = HBW x 20

Examples:

HEIGHT	HBW*	BMR	CALORIE NEEDS		
			LIGHT ACTIVITY	MODERATE ACTIVITY	HEAVY ACTIVITY
5'0"	97-128	970-1280	1455-1920	1649-2176	1940-2560
5'2"	104-136	1040-1360	1560-2040	1768-2312	2080-2720
5'4"	110-145	1100-1450	1650-2175	1870-2465	2200-2900
5'6"	118-155	1180-1550	1770-2325	2006-2635	2360-3100
5'8"	125-164	1250-1640	1875-2460	2125-2788	2500-3280
5'10"	132-174	1320-1740	1980-2610	2244-2958	2640-3480
6'0"	140-184	1400-1840	2100-2760	2380-3128	2800-3680
6'2"	148-194	1480-1940	2220-2910	2516-3298	2960-3880

*Healthy Body Weight is based on a Body Mass Index of 19-25

FOOD DESCRIPTION	SERVING SIZE	WATER (%)	CALORIES (kcal)	PROTEIN (g)	TOTAL FAT (g)	SATURATED (g)	MONO UNSATURATED (g)	POLY UNSATURATED (g)	CHOLESTEROL (mg)	CARBOHYDRATE (g)	TOTAL DIETARY FIBER (g)	CALCIUM (mg)	IRON (mg)	POTASSIUM (mg)	SODIUM (mg)	VITAMIN A (mg)	THIAMIN (mg)	RIBOFLAVIN (mg)	NIACIN (mg)	ASCORBIC ACID (mg)
Cola	12 fl oz	89	152	0	0	0.0	0.0	0.0	0	Tr	0.0	14	0.1	0	21	0	0.02	0.08	0.0	0
Coffee, black	6 fl oz	99	4	Tr	0	Tr	0.0	Tr	0	1	0.0	4	0.1	96	4	0	0.00	0.00	0.4	0
White sugar	1 tsp	0	16	0	0	0.0	0.0	0.0	0	4	0.0	Tr	Tr	Tr	Tr	0	0.00	Tr	0.0	0
Half and half	1 tbsp	81	20	Tr	2	1.1	0.5	0.1	6	1	0.0	16	Tr	19	6	65	0.01	0.02	Tr	Tr
Apple juice	1 cup	88	117	Tr	Tr	Tr	Tr	0.1	0	29	0.2	17	0.9	295	7	2	0.05	0.04	0.2	2
Orange juice, frozen	1 cup	88	112	2	Tr	Tr	Tr	Tr	0	27	0.5	22	0.2	473	2	194	0.20	0.04	0.5	97
Apple (2 1/2" dia)	1 apple	84	81	Tr	Tr	0.1	Tr	0.1	0	21	3.7	10	0.2	159	0	73	0.02	0.02	0.1	8
Banana	1 medium	74	109	1	1	0.2	Tr	Tr	0	28	2.8	7	0.4	467	1	96	0.05	0.12	0.6	11
Orange (2 1/2" dia)	1 orange	87	62	1	Tr	Tr	Tr	Tr	0	15	3.1	52	0.1	237	0	269	0.11	0.05	0.4	70
Whole egg	1 large	75	75	6	5	1.6	1.9	0.7	213	1	0.0	25	0.7	61	63	318	0.03	0.25	Tr	0
Egg substitute, liquid	1/4 cup	83	53	8	2	0.4	0.6	1.0	1	Tr	0.0	33	1.3	208	112	1,361	0.07	0.19	0.1	15
Cheerios	1 cup	3	110	3	2	0.4	0.6	0.2	0	23	2.6	55	8.1	89	284	1,250	0.38	0.43	5.0	0
Cap'n Crunch	3/4 cup	2	107	1	1	0.4	0.3	0.2	0	23	0.9	5	4.5	35	208	36	0.38	0.42	5.0	0
Bagel, plain	3 1/2" bagel	33	195	7	1	0.2	0.1	0.5	0	38	1.6	53	2.5	72	379	0	0.21	0.22	3.2	Tr
Biscuit	2 1/2" biscuit	29	212	4	10	2.6	4.2	2.5	2	27	0.9	141	1.7	73	348	49	0.10	0.19	1.8	0
Bread, wheat	1 slice	37	65	2	1	0.2	0.4	0.2	0	12	1.1	26	0.8	50	133	0	0.12	0.07	1.0	0
Bread, white	1 slice	37	67	2	1	0.1	0.2	0.5	Tr	12	0.6	27	0.8	30	135	0	0.12	0.09	1.0	0
Butter, salted	1 tsp	16	36	Tr	4	2.5	1.2	0.2	11	Tr	0.0	1	Tr	1	41	153	Tr	Tr	Tr	0
Bologna	2 slices	54	180	7	16	6.1	7.6	1.4	31	2	0.0	7	0.9	103	581	0	0.10	0.08	1.5	0
Hot dog	1 frank	45	144	5	13	4.8	6.2	1.2	23	1	0.0	5	0.5	75	504	0	0.09	0.05	1.2	0
Hamburger 83% lean	3 oz	57	218	22	14	5.5	6.1	0.5	71	0	0.0	6	2.0	266	60	0	0.05	0.23	4.2	0
Cheeseburger	1 single	48	295	16	14	6.3	5.3	1.1	37	27	NA	111	2.4	223	616	462	0.25	0.23	3.7	2
Chicken nuggets	6 pieces	47	319	18	21	4.7	10.5	4.6	61	15	0.0	14	0.9	305	513	0	0.12	0.16	7.5	0
Fish stick, frozen	1 portion	46	155	9	7	1.8	2.9	1.8	64	14	0.0	11	0.4	149	332	60	0.07	0.10	1.2	0
Tuna in water	3 oz	85	99	22	1	0.2	0.1	0.3	26	0	0.0	9	1.3	201	287	48	0.03	0.06	11.3	0
Sirloin steak	3 oz	57	219	24	13	5.2	5.6	0.5	77	0	0.0	9	2.6	311	54	0	0.09	0.23	3.3	0
Regular bacon	3 slices	13	109	6	9	3.3	4.5	1.1	16	Tr	0.0	2	0.3	92	303	0	0.13	0.05	1.4	0
French fries	Medium	35	458	6	25	5.2	14.3	4.2	0	53	4.7	19	1.0	923	265	0	0.11	0.05	3.8	16
Potato chips, regular	1 oz	2	152	2	10	3.1	2.8	3.5	0	15	1.3	7	0.5	361	168	0	0.05	0.06	1.1	9
Potato, baked	1 medium	71	220	5	Tr	0.1	Tr	0.1	0	51	4.8	20	2.7	844	16	0	0.22	0.07	3.3	26
Whole kernel corn, can	1 cup	77	166	5	1	0.2	0.3	0.5	0	41	4.2	11	0.9	391	571	506	0.09	0.15	2.5	17
Lettuce (iceberg)	1 cup	96	7	Tr	Tr	Tr	Tr	0.1	0	1	0.8	10	0.3	87	5	182	0.03	0.02	0.1	2
Baby carrot	1 medium	90	4	Tr	Tr	Tr	Tr	Tr	0	1	0.2	2	0.1	28	4	1,501	Tr	0.01	0.1	1
Italian dressing	1 tbsp	38	69	Tr	7	1.0	1.6	4.1	0	1	0.0	1	Tr	2	116	11	Tr	Tr	Tr	0
Mayonnaise	1 tbsp	15	99	Tr	11	1.6	3.1	5.7	8	Tr	0.0	2	0.1	5	78	39	0.00	0.00	Tr	0
Chocolate frozen yogurt	1/2 cup	64	115	3	4	2.6	1.3	0.2	4	18	1.6	106	0.9	188	71	115	0.03	0.15	0.2	Tr
Chocolate ice cream	1/2 cup	56	143	3	7	4.5	2.1	0.3	22	19	0.8	72	0.6	164	50	275	0.03	0.13	0.1	Tr
Whole almonds	24 nuts	5	164	6	14	1.1	9.1	3.5	0	6	3.3	70	1.2	206	Tr	3	0.07	0.23	1.1	Tr
Peanuts, roasted, salted	1 oz	2	165	7	14	1.9	6.9	4.4	0	5	2.6	25	0.5	193	123	0	0.07	0.03	4.0	0
M&M's plain	1/4 cup	2	256	2	11	6.8	3.6	0.3	7	37	1.3	55	0.6	138	32	106	0.03	0.11	0.1	Tr

person eats in a day is his or her caloric intake. This is the figure we use in evaluating dietary intake, even if some of the nutrients are used as raw material for building muscle.

Different classes of nutrients provide different amounts of calories. Carbohydrates and proteins can each provide 4 calories per gram. Fat can provide 9 calories per gram. Thus, ten grams of protein provides 40 calories.

A snack containing eight grams of fat and seven grams of carbohydrates provides 100 calories. Why? Because 8 x 9 = 72, and 7 x 4 = 28, for a total of 100 calories.

A protein bar consisting of 7 grams of fat, 41 grams of carbohydrate, and 10 grams of protein provides (7 x 9) + (41 x 4) + (10 x 4) = 267 calories of quick nutritious energy.

ENERGY SUPPLIED IN CALORIES	
Carbohydrate	4 calories per gram
Protein	4 calories per gram
Fat	9 calories per gram
Alcohol	7 calories per gram

RECOMMENDED CALORIE DISTRIBUTION	
Carbohydrate	45-65%
Protein	10-35%
Fat	20-35%

TAKING A CLOSER LOOK
Nutritional Labels

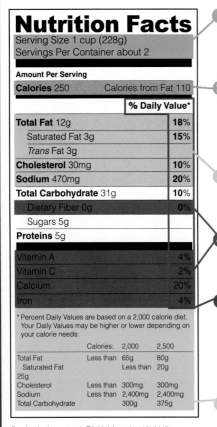

① Serving Size
This section is the basis for determining number of calories, amount of each nutrient, and %DVs of a food. Use it to compare a serving size to how much you actually eat. Serving sizes are given in familiar units, such as cups or pieces, followed by the metric amount, e.g., number of grams.

② Amount of Calories
If you want to manage your weight (lose, gain, or maintain), this section is especially helpful. The amount of calories is listed on the left side. The right side shows how many calories in one serving come from fat. In this example, there are 250 calories, 110 of which come from fat. The key is to balance how many calories you eat with how many calories your body uses. Tip: Remember that a product that's fat-free isn't necessarily calorie-free.

③ Limit these Nutrients
Eating too much total fat (including saturated fat and trans fat), cholesterol, or sodium may increase your risk of certain chronic diseases, such as heart disease, some cancers, or high blood pressure. The goal is to stay below 100%DV for each of these nutrients per day.

④ Get Enough of these Nutrients
Americans often don't get enough dietary fiber, vitamin A, vitamin C, calcium, and iron in their diets. Eating enough of these nutrients may improve your health and help reduce the risk of some diseases and conditions.

⑤ Percent (%) Daily Value
This section tells you whether the nutrients (total fat, sodium, dietary fiber, etc.) in one serving of food contribute a little or a lot to your total daily diet. The %DVs are based on a 2,000-calorie diet. Each listed nutrient is based on 100% of the recommended amounts for that nutrient. For example, 18% for total fat means that one serving furnishes 18% of the total amount of fat that you could eat in a day and stay within public health recommendations.

⑥ Footnote with Daily Values (DVs)
The footnote provides information about the DVs for important nutrients, including fats, sodium, and fiber. The DVs are listed for people who eat 2,000 or 2,500 calories each day. The amounts for total fat, saturated fat, cholesterol, and sodium are maximum amounts. That means you should try to stay below the amounts listed.

But it is not just the total number of calories per day that needs to be considered in choosing a healthy diet. What is the correct proportion of macronutrients in the best-balanced diet? The answer varies according to whom you ask.

Over the years, there have been differing opinions about the make-up of an ideal diet. Some experts say that about 60 percent of calories need to come from carbohydrates, 20 percent from proteins, and 20 percent from fats. Others suggest it needs to be more like 70 percent carbohydrates, 20 percent proteins, and only 10 percent fats. Still others say only about 50 percent carbohydrates, 35 percent protein, and 15 percent fats. This gets more than a little confusing. And when advocates of fad diets put in their two cents, these numbers are all over the place.

Obesity

Obesity is a condition where a person's body weight is high enough that it adversely affects his or her health. Obesity comes down to one thing: too much adipose tissue (body fat).

Obesity is an all-too-common problem today. It has been estimated that 90 million people in the United States are obese. Given our modern diet and our sedentary lifestyles, we should not really be surprised at this number.

Obesity is, as mentioned, an excess of body fat. One of the most common methods for estimating this is the body mass index (BMI). A normal BMI is 18 to 25. A BMI over 30 indicates obesity.

People who are obese are at higher risk for a variety of diseases and illnesses. These include type 2 diabetes, high blood pressure, sleep apnea, heart disease, asthma, gallstones, among many others. This is tragic because obesity is generally preventable and correctable.

The most obvious first line of intervention for obesity is a sensible regimen of diet and exercise. This is often done with the help of a skilled dietitian who can help identify and correct poor dietary habits. Proper routines of exercise can be laid out. A physician's assessment includes tests to search for any medical conditions that exacerbate obesity or that obesity has caused. Follow-up with a physician can monitor the person's progress, watch for any changes in overall health, and provide encouragement. In certain situations, temporary extreme regulation of dietary intake or even medications may be given to aid with weight loss. Patients on these diets and medications must be closely monitored for any adverse effects. In the most extreme cases, surgical intervention, such as surgical procedures that diminish the amount of food a person may comfortably eat, may be recommended to achieve the needed weight loss.

Regardless of the methods used to help a person achieve an ideal weight, he or she must learn healthier eating habits and make them a permanent part of their lives. Likewise, for many obese people, a regular exercise regimen represents a drastic change. While the road to obesity always involves the consumption of more calories than the body burns through activity, the root causes of any individual's obesity may vary. Likewise, victory over obesity may take many different routes. But maintaining that hard-won victory requires some permanent lifestyle changes that will help a person limit his or her consumption to healthy foods in amounts that do not exceed the calories burned through activity and exercise.

It seems reasonable that the majority of calories should generally come from carbohydrates, say about 65 percent. After all, carbohydrates have many uses in the body. First and foremost, they are the body's primary source of energy. So we need carbohydrates. Yet, it turns out that not all carbohydrates are of equal value for your health. Remember, you are better off eating more complex carbohydrates and limiting your consumption of sugars. For now, let's just say your pancreas will thank you. And you should already know that your teeth will thank you!

We also need proteins. The amino acids we obtain from proteins provide the building blocks for the growth and repair of the body. If you wish to become stronger and build more muscle through any sort of training regimen, you certainly need to provide your body with plenty of protein.

Body Mass Index

Doctors are always looking for techniques to assess people's risk factors for disease. That helps us predict who is more likely to suffer from particular illnesses. It also helps us advise people about what they can do to lessen their risks. Doing blood tests to check for cholesterol or blood sugar levels, monitoring blood pressure, testing for the presence of heart disease — all these things help the doctor take good care of the patient.

A big issue in the last few decades is obesity. It is clear that the more overweight you are, the more your risk for certain diseases increases. That's all well and good, but how obese is obese? How do you determine exactly how fat a person really is?

It turns out that it's not all that easy. One method in common use is called the body mass index (BMI). The BMI is an estimate of a person's body fat based on his or her height and weight. That does make some sense, right? After all, a five-foot tall person weighing 250 pounds should have more body fat than a six-and-a-half-foot tall person weighing 250 pounds. That just seems logical.

So how does it work? Take your weight in pounds and divide that number by your height in inches squared. Then take that number and multiply it by 703. (I'm not making this up. Doctors actually do this . . . or else they look it up on a chart).

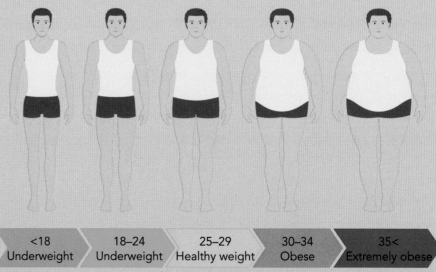

<18 Underweight	18–24 Underweight	25–29 Healthy weight	30–34 Obese	35< Extremely obese

A body mass index for a normal person at their healthy weight should be between 18 and 25. A person with a BMI between 25 and 30 would be considered overweight. A person with a BMI over 30 would be considered obese.

You must understand that this is just a means for estimating obesity. It is by no means perfect. For example, the BMI can be fooled by a weight-lifter or a highly trained athlete with a larger than normal muscle mass. Their extra weight is muscle and not fat. Therefore, their BMI would calculate high, but they are not overweight.

Plus, despite the bad reputation fats get, we do need to consume some fat. However, most people eat too much fat. Too much fat can put a person at a higher risk of heart disease and other health problems.

So, at the end of the day, the best diet is a balanced one. Get your carbohydrates every day. Make sure to get enough protein. You will almost certainly get a little fat in there, too, if you eat anything at all.

One of the best ways to "balance" your diet is to eat a variety of foods from several food groups. Many experts have suggested ways to do this. You've probably seen food pyramids. A food pyramid was a triangular diagram built of layers representing the servings of different types of foods thought desirable in a healthy diet. The bottom layer represented the sorts of foods you needed to eat more of, such as breads and cereals. The next layer up held pictures of fruits and vegetables. Next up came dairy products and other high protein foods like meat and eggs. And at the top, to discourage eating too much junk food, were fats and sugar.

The United States Department of Agriculture used to publish food pyramids to educate people about nutrition. It would revise the food pyramid every few years to reflect the latest scientific research. Now, all versions of the food pyramid have been retired. But the concept that a balanced diet should include a variety of healthy foods is still a good one. To reflect that, the USDA has published simpler guidelines called MyPlate.

Body Mass Index Chart

Weight / Height	100	105	110	115	120	125	130	135	140	145	150	155	160	165	170	175	180	185	190	195	200	205	210	215
5'0"	19	20	21	22	23	24	25	26	27	28	29	30	31	32	33	34	35	36	37	38	39	40	41	42
5'1"	18	19	20	21	22	23	24	25	26	27	28	29	30	31	32	33	34	35	36	36	37	38	39	40
5'2"	18	19	20	21	22	22	23	24	25	26	27	28	29	30	31	32	33	33	34	35	36	37	38	39
5'3"	17	18	19	20	21	22	23	24	24	25	26	27	28	29	30	31	32	32	33	34	35	36	37	38
5'4"	17	18	18	19	20	21	22	23	24	24	25	26	27	28	29	30	31	31	32	33	34	35	36	37
5'5"	16	17	18	19	20	20	21	22	23	24	25	25	26	27	28	29	30	30	31	32	33	34	35	35
5'6"	16	17	17	18	19	20	21	21	22	23	24	25	25	26	27	28	29	29	30	31	32	33	34	34
5'7"	15	16	17	18	18	19	20	21	22	22	23	24	25	25	26	27	28	29	29	30	31	32	33	33
5'8"	15	16	16	17	18	19	19	20	21	22	22	23	24	25	25	26	27	28	28	29	30	31	32	32
5'9"	14	15	16	17	17	18	19	20	20	21	22	22	23	24	25	25	26	27	28	28	29	30	31	31
5'10"	14	15	15	16	17	18	18	19	20	20	21	22	23	23	24	25	25	26	27	28	28	29	30	30
5'11"	14	14	15	16	16	17	18	18	19	20	21	21	22	23	23	24	25	25	26	27	28	28	29	30
6'0"	13	14	14	15	16	17	17	18	19	19	20	21	21	22	23	23	24	25	25	26	27	27	28	29
6'1"	13	13	14	15	15	16	17	17	18	19	19	20	21	21	22	23	23	24	25	25	26	27	27	28
6'2"	12	13	14	14	15	16	16	17	18	18	19	19	20	21	21	22	23	23	24	25	25	26	27	27
6'3"	12	13	13	14	15	15	16	16	17	18	18	19	20	20	21	22	22	23	23	24	25	25	26	26
6'4"	12	12	13	14	14	15	15	16	17	17	18	18	19	20	20	21	22	22	23	23	24	25	25	26

A standard body mass index chart

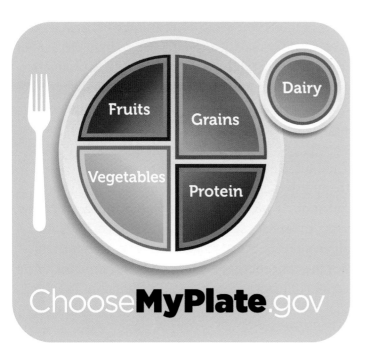

MyPlate is simply a picture suggesting our daily diet should consist of about half vegetables and fruits and about half grains and proteins, plus some dairy products. Whole grains are healthier choices than highly processed ones. Healthier meat choices should lean toward leaner meats. The more you vary the particular vegetables and fruits, grains and proteins, the more balanced your diet will be because you will make up for the occasional lack of a nutrient by getting it in another food at another time. Limiting the amounts of fats and sugars continues to be a good idea. As to specific proportions, expert recommendations still vary a lot and will doubtless continue to change as new research reveals more about the complex interaction between our bodies and the foods it takes to keep us at our best.

By the way, there's nothing wrong with having a hot fudge sundae . . . but only every now and then.

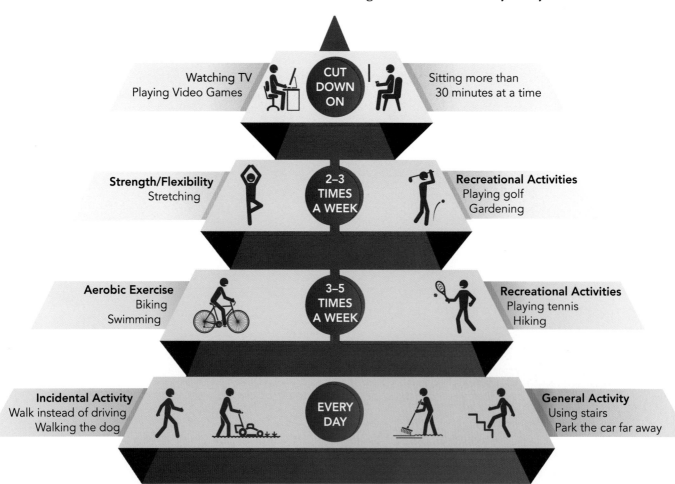

What Is Metabolism?

Up to this point, we have seen how the materials in our food are broken down into their molecular components and absorbed. But what about those tiny components? What happens next? How are the building blocks of all those nutrients used? Glad you asked. Here goes. . . .

Here begins our study of metabolism. *Metabolism* simply means all the biochemical reactions that occur in the body to keep us alive. Chemical reactions transform one kind of molecule into another. Some of those chemical reactions build proteins like enzymes or the components of muscle tissue. Some break down proteins to get energy or the raw materials to make other things. Some reactions need energy. Some produce usable energy. There are a lot of reactions, and most of them have many steps, so let's make it easier. There are two types of metabolism — anabolism and catabolism. Just two. *Anabolic reactions* are those processes that take simpler molecules and build them into larger molecules or structures. *Anabolism* is building up. *Catabolic reactions*, as you might expect, are processes in which larger molecules or substances are broken down into smaller or simpler ones. *Catabolism* is breaking down.

If metabolism includes all the chemical processes in the body, that's pretty much everything, right? Seems like an awfully big topic to cover. That is quite true. In fact, to cover the majority of the metabolic processes in the body would require several large textbooks. (Remember this sentence when you get to medical school!) We are not going to be quite so ambitious here. Our focus will be to examine a few of the metabolic processes involving carbohydrates, proteins, and fats.

How do the cells in your body control all these reactions? That's where enzymes come in. *Enzymes* are proteins that *catalyze*, or speed up, a chemical reaction. Practically speaking, biochemical reactions happen in living organisms as directed by the enzymes present. Every step in these chemical reactions, whether catabolic or anabolic, is generally controlled by an enzyme. And enzymes are produced at the instructions of the DNA in a cell.

Carbohydrate Metabolism

The goal of carbohydrate digestion is to secure an adequate supply of monosaccharides, primarily glucose. Many substances in the body can be used as a source of fuel, but by far glucose is the most important. Therefore, glucose will be our focus here.

After glucose is absorbed by the small intestine, it is transported to the liver by the portal vein. After reaching the liver, one of two things can happen. The glucose can continue in the circulation for use as fuel by cells all over the body, or it can be taken up by the liver or skeletal muscles and stored for future needs.

In times of lower energy requirements, hormone signals sent to the liver indicate that all the glucose is not immediately needed. Some of the excess glucose is taken into the hepatocytes, and these glucose molecules are linked together with other glucose molecules to form a highly branched polysaccharide called *glycogen*. Glycogen is the only storage form of carbohydrate in the human body. About 75 percent of glycogen is stored in skeletal muscle and 25 percent remains stored in the liver. At times when energy requirements are high, glycogen can be broken down into glucose and utilized.

Most glucose finds its way out to the cells of the body. The glucose is taken into the cells by means of special transport proteins in the plasma membrane. Once inside the cell, a reaction occurs that links a phosphate group to the glucose molecule. This newly formed glucose-phosphate molecule cannot then be taken back out of the cell.

The glucose inside the cell is then metabolized by a number of different biochemical reactions. All of these different reactions are part of a process called *cellular respiration*. Simply understood, these are all the processes that produce ATP, the body's energy molecule. The two aspects of glucose metabolism we will examine are *aerobic respiration* and *anaerobic respiration*.

Aerobic respiration is the metabolism of glucose to produce ATP in the presence of oxygen (hence "aerobic"). Let's go through the process.

The initial step of aerobic respiration is called *glycolysis* (*Glycose* is an older word for glucose sugar, and *-lysis* means "break or cut"). Each glucose molecule is split into two smaller molecules of *pyruvic acid*. Glycolysis actually uses two molecules of ATP in its initial step, but ultimately it produces

Adenosine Triphosphate

One of the most important molecules in the body is *adenosine triphosphate*. It is most commonly known as *ATP*. The bonds in ATP molecules store the usable energy produced by many metabolic processes.

ATP is made up of a purine molecule called *adenine* and a molecule of the sugar *ribose*. Attached to the ribose portion are three phosphate groups (PO_4). It is in the bonds between these phosphate groups that energy can be stored.

In the cell, the precursor of ATP is adenosine diphosphate (ADP). This molecule has only two phosphate groups (hence "*diphosphate*"). When glucose is metabolized, energy is released. This energy is used to join another phosphate group to ADP, thus producing ATP. This process allows the body to have energy in a usable from.

There are many processes in the body that require energy. ATP is vital to these processes. Without ATP, there is no energy for them to happen.

When energy is needed, a phosphate group is removed from the ATP. The result is ADP plus the removed phosphate group. Plus energy! So basically, what is seen here is the reverse of what we saw previously. Here the ATP is broken down to ADP and energy is released. When ATP is made from ADP, energy is required.

An easy way of thinking about this is to consider the cycle like a rechargeable battery. Producing ATP is like the charging of the battery. It takes energy. Then the breaking down of ATP into ADP is like using the battery. It releases energy! And this process continues, over and over. ATP is being made and utilized constantly.

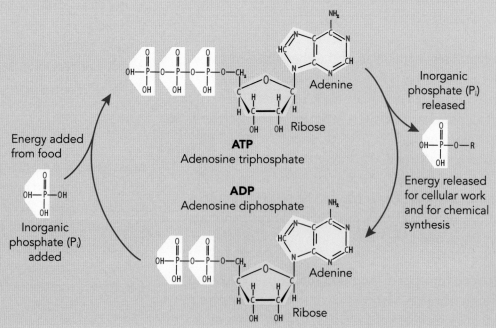

four molecules of ATP by the time pyruvic acid is formed. Thus, there is a total gain of two ATP molecules. Glycolysis takes place in the cytoplasm of a cell.

Next, pyruvic acid molecules are transported into mitochondria. Remember, the *mitochondria* are the energy-producing organelles — the powerhouses — of the cell. Cells with higher energy needs tend to have more mitochondria. In the mitochondria, the pyruvic acid undergoes further transformation and enters the *citric acid cycle* (sometimes called the *Krebs cycle*). This is a series of 8 different reactions that occur in the matrix of the mitochondria. The citric acid cycle produces several by-products that are themselves processed by special proteins (called the electron transport chain) on the inner wall of the

mitochondria. At the end of all these reactions you have water, carbon dioxide, and a lot of ATP! Every molecule of glucose metabolized this way yields 2 ATP through glycolysis plus 30 ATP molecules through the citric acid cycle and the electron transport chain. Quite an efficient process, don't you think?

Just think about this for a moment. Is there really any way you can convince yourself that this incredibly complex chain of reactions just happened by accident? It looks like the work of an amazing Designer.

But what if there isn't a lot of oxygen around? For example, a person sprinting or doing an intense weightlifting session might become temporarily short of oxygen. Fortunately, in these situations the body can still produce energy. At least for a while. This is where anaerobic respiration occurs. Here, metabolism occurs in the absence of oxygen.

I know you must be thinking, here we go with another set of reactions. Well, no. You are due some good news, and here it is. You already know the pathway! It's just glycolysis. Remember, glucose enters the cell and is metabolized into pyruvic acid. That reaction produced a net gain of two ATP molecules. That is all anaerobic respiration is, glycolysis. You see, the other reaction cycles in aerobic respiration need oxygen, so those cycles don't function in its absence. So, all you have without oxygen is glycolysis alone. It is not very efficient, as you can see. It only produces two molecules of ATP for each glucose molecule. Also, the by-products of glycolysis are not water and carbon dioxide. The by-product of glycolysis

Metabolism – Where do the calories go?

An average resting adult uses about 70% of the calories consumed simply to stay alive. This is called the resting metabolic rate. These calories are necessary for essential body functions. They supply the energy to keep the heart, lungs, liver, kidneys, and brain working. Another 10% is used to digest food. That leaves around 20% to power the muscles for ordinary, non-exercise sorts of activities.

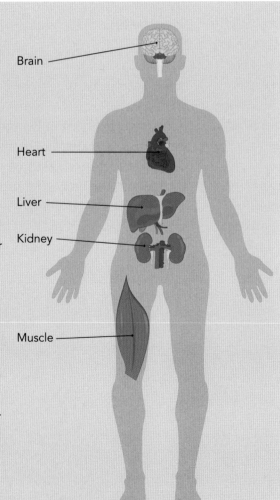

Brain

Heart

Liver

Kidney

Muscle

is lactic acid. Lactic acid can build up in muscles if anaerobic respiration continues too long. It can make muscles cramp and become fatigued. Once sufficient oxygen enters the cells, the lactic acid can be carried away and aerobic respiration can resume.

Let's picture then what happens in a muscle in a sprinter. Muscles store glycogen. They make this glycogen when glucose is available. If an athlete's training depletes muscle glycogen, when he or she is resting and resupplying the body with good nutrition, the muscle glycogen is replenished and even topped off with a little more. Training also improves the blood flow and oxygen delivery to the muscles. On the day of the big race, a well-trained athlete's muscles have lots of glycogen stored up, and the athlete's cardiovascular system delivers plenty of oxygen to the muscles. While racing, the three processes of aerobic respiration — glycolysis, the citric acid cycle, and the electron transport chain — take place using glucose molecules nipped off of the muscle glycogen. The athlete is able to get the maximum amount of energy possible from his or her muscles, generating the speed and endurance needed to finish the race and make a good showing.

If an untrained person ran the same race, he or she would not have as much glycogen stored in the muscles. And the muscles would not have as sufficient a supply of oxygen from the untrained cardiovascular system. Soon after starting the sprint, the untrained athlete would be huffing and puffing, trying to get more oxygen for those aching leg muscles. His or her legs would be fatigued and cramping. Why? Because without sufficient oxygen, aerobic respiration would have to stop, leaving only glycolysis — anaerobic respiration — to produce energy. Not nearly as much energy — only 2 ATP instead of 32 ATP — is produced from each glucose molecule. Meanwhile, the meager glycogen stores would soon be exhausted, and our untrained racer would be lucky to finish the race at a run and would do so with lots of leg cramps due to the lactic acid accumulating in the muscles.

Lipid Metabolism

We tend to think of fats as something bad. After all, when we take in too many calories, we may become fat.

When we eat too much, the body can make triglycerides with the excess calories. Whether we take in too many carbohydrates, proteins, or fats, any type of excess calories can ultimately be converted into triglycerides and stored in adipose tissue throughout the body. The process of converting nutrients into triglycerides is called *lipogenesis* (*lipo-* meaning "fat" or "lipid," *-genesis* meaning "creation" or "origin"). This is actually a very efficient method

of storing energy. Remember that carbohydrates and proteins have only 4 calories per gram. Fats have 9 calories per gram. Lots of calories are stored in our adipose tissue. Imagine how much more room on our hips and tummies would be required if excess fuel were stored as protein or carbohydrate: at least twice as much!

The reverse of lipogenesis is *lipolysis*. This is the breaking down of fats, mainly triglycerides. As you recall, triglycerides are a combination of one molecule of glycerol and three fatty acid chains. When these molecules are broken down by enzymes called lipases, the triglyceride can then be metabolized. The glycerol molecule is often metabolized by glycolysis. The fatty acids are broken down into a form that can enter the citric acid cycle. The remainder of aerobic respiration proceeds from that point, gaining usable energy from the metabolism of fat molecules.

Protein Metabolism

Amino acids are constantly being used to build new proteins. This is simply protein anabolism. Here, smaller units, the amino acids, are being used to construct bigger things, the proteins. We have already seen examples of this. The enzymes that digest our food are themselves proteins and must be built from amino acids and replaced as they wear out. If you train to build stronger, bigger muscles, you hope that the extra protein you consume will be used to provide the amino acids to build up the muscles you have been exercising.

Less commonly considered is protein catabolism. Here we have the breaking down of larger units into smaller ones. Tissues wear out; injuries occur. These worn out or damaged tissues are commonly recycled. The tissues are basically disassembled into their component amino acids, and the amino acids are reused as new or replacement proteins are synthesized.

Also, protein can be catabolized into amino acids for another purpose. This purpose is for the amino acids to be used for energy. Amino acids can be modified for use in cellular respiration. It is also possible to use amino acids in a process that ultimately results in the production of new glucose molecules.

However, it is really not beneficial for protein to be used as a primary source of energy. Proteins are our main structural component. Even though proteins and carbohydrates both have 4 calories per gram, proteins are not as well-suited for energy production as carbohydrates. It is only in situations where there is extreme calorie deprivation that large amounts of protein are used for energy. Think of the use of proteins for energy as a backup arrangement for emergencies. God our Designer thought of everything, even the problems that would occur in a sin-cursed world. We are indeed wonderfully made.

We have come to the end of another amazing study.

Just stop and think of where we have been. We examined all the organs of the digestive system. Because of this intricate and incredibly coordinated set of organs, our food can be turned into the energy we need.

We learned about the various classes of nutrients and why each of them is vital to the proper function of the body. How amazing are all those reactions that turn our nutrients into energy!

We even examined how important diet is to our physical well-being.

But there is one more thing. There is something about diet that is even more important. It is important to our spiritual well-being.

Let's end with a lesson from Genesis. . . .

5

A LESSON FROM GENESIS

In the beginning God created the heavens and the earth.

(Genesis 1:1)

In the very first verse of the Bible, we are told something marvelous. God created the heavens and the earth. You see, here in this first verse God tells us something about Himself. He is the One who created.

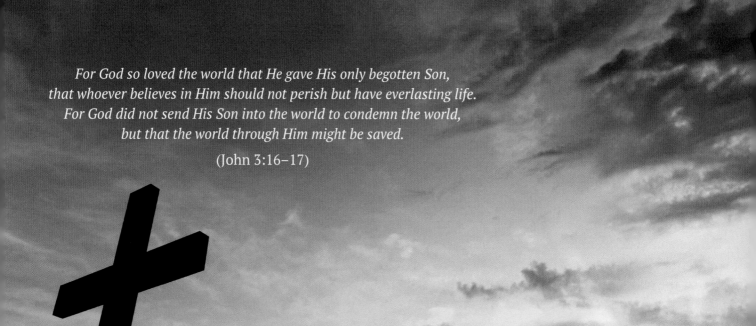

For God so loved the world that He gave His only begotten Son, that whoever believes in Him should not perish but have everlasting life. For God did not send His Son into the world to condemn the world, but that the world through Him might be saved.

(John 3:16–17)

As we read further in Genesis, we find that on the first day, He created earth, space, time, and light. On the second day, He separated the waters from the waters. On the third day, He created the dry land and plants. On the fourth day, He put the sun, moon, planets, and stars in their places. On the fifth day, He created the flying and sea creatures. On the sixth day, He created the land animals and man.

And we are also told . . .

And God said, "See, I have given you every herb that yields seed which is on the face of all the earth, and every tree whose fruit yields seed; to you it shall be for food. Also, to every beast of the earth, to every bird of the air, and to everything that creeps on the earth, in which there is life, I have given every green herb for food"; and it was so.

(Genesis 1:29–30)

In the beginning, man and the animals were given plants to eat. You see, animals did not kill each other for food. People did not kill animals for food. In the beginning, there was no animal death. Can you imagine a world without death? It was like that in the beginning.

And when He finished creating, He looked on everything He had made and said it was "very good."

His communication to us is direct and specific. He tells us what He did and when He did it. Why is that important? It is very important.

Is Evolution True?

We are not just products of chance, the result of millions of years of chemicals banging into one another. Everything we see around us did not just "happen." These things did not create themselves. You see, if evolution is true, then there could not have been a time when there was no death. If evolution is true, then death has been here for

millions of years. God's Word tells us evolution cannot be true.

Then Why is There Death?

Our Creator made for us a perfect creation where there was no death. To keep it, all we had to do was obey Him. Man could obey or disobey:

And the Lord God commanded the man, saying, "Of every tree of the garden you may freely eat; but of the tree of the knowledge of good and evil you shall not eat, for in the day that you eat of it you shall surely die."

(Genesis 2:16–17)

Man disobeyed God by taking of the tree of the knowledge of good and evil. It was then that death came into the world. God's perfect creation was broken. What broke it, you ask? Our sin broke it, simple as that.

What Does All This Mean to Me?

This is important to us all because death comes to all men. It comes to all men because of our sin, our rebellion against our Creator God:

Therefore, just as through one man sin entered the world, and death through sin, and thus death spread to all men, because all sinned.

(Romans 5:12)

Can any of us truly say that we have not sinned? No, we cannot. We have all sinned, and our sin makes us worthy of death.

But we don't have to take the punishment that is rightfully ours. God in His mercy has provided a substitute, One who has taken upon Himself the sins of the world. All you need do is repent of your sins and place your faith and trust in the One who is worthy, our Lord and Savior Jesus Christ. Trust Him today.

GLOSSARY

Absorption — the movement of the products of digestion into the cells lining the GI tract

Accessory digestive organs — the digestive organs outside the gastrointestinal tract itself; these are the teeth, tongue, salivary glands, liver, gallbladder, and pancreas

Adenosine triphosphate (ATP) — a molecule that stores energy needed for metabolic processes

Aerobic respiration — the metabolism of glucose into ATP in the presence of oxygen

Alimentary canal — another term for the gastrointestinal tract; the tubular portion of the digestive system

Amino acids — the basic building blocks of proteins; there are 20 different amino acids in the body

Anabolism — the process of taking smaller things and building larger things; for example, amino acids being used to build proteins is an example of anabolism

Anaerobic respiration — the metabolism of glucose into ATP in the absence of oxygen

Appendicitis — inflammation of the appendix

Bile — a secretory product of the liver used in the digestion of lipids

Body mass index (BMI) — a method of estimating a person's level of body fat based on his or her height and weight

Calorie — the amount of energy needed to raise one kilogram of water by one degree centigrade; this refers to a "dietary" or "food" calorie; a dietary calorie is 1,000 times larger than a standard calorie

Carbohydrates — substances we commonly refer to as sugars and starches; their primary use in the body is as a source of energy

Catabolism — the process of larger things being broken down into smaller things; for example, the recycling of worn out proteins into their component amino acids is an example of catabolism

Cavity — a hole in the enamel of a tooth

Cellular respiration — the processes that produce ATP, the body's energy molecule

Chemical digestion — the breaking down of food into its more basic components by digestive enzymes

Chief cell — a cell in the stomach that secretes pepsinogen

Chyme — the mass of partially digested material that passes from the stomach into the small intestine

Dental caries — tooth decay

Digestion — the process by which the food we take in is converted into substances needed by the body

Elimination — the removal of indigestible material from the GI tract

Endoscope — a fiber-optic instrument used to view the lining of the GI tract

Enteric nervous system — neurons in the walls of the GI tract that help regulate the digestive process

Enterohepatic circulation — the process by which bile salts are recycled

Esophagus — the muscular tube that connects the pharynx to the stomach

Essential amino acids — amino acids that cannot be synthesized by the body; these amino acids must be provided by dietary intake

Essential nutrient — something the body either cannot make on its own, or cannot make fast enough, to meet the body's needs

Gallbladder — a small sac-like accessory digestive organ that stores bile

Gastrointestinal (GI) tract — the tubular portion of the digestive system; it extends from the mouth to the anus

Gingivitis — inflammation of the gums

Gland — an organ that secretes useful chemical substances

Glycogen — a polysaccharide made of glucose molecules; it is used by the body to store energy

Halitosis — chronic bad breath

Hepatitis — inflammation of the liver

Hepatocyte — the primary cell type found in the liver

Ingestion — taking food into the GI tract

Large intestine — the final portion of the GI tract; it consists of the cecum, ascending colon, transverse colon, descending colon, sigmoid colon, and rectum

Laryngopharynx — the portion of the pharynx from the end of the oropharynx down to the esophagus

Lipids — several types of compounds including fatty acids, triglycerides, phospholipids, and steroids; sometimes lipids are simply called fats

Liver — a large gland located in the right upper quadrant of the abdomen; it is an accessory digestive organ that has several hundred functions in the body

Macronutrients — the types of nutrients that the body needs in large amounts; these are the things needed for production of energy and the building of tissues

Mastication — chewing

Mechanical digestion — the process of tearing, grinding, and churning of food in order to break larger pieces into smaller ones

Metabolism — all the biochemical reactions that occur in the body to keep us alive

Micronutrients — types of nutrients needed by the body, but in small amounts

Mineral — a chemical element (a micronutrient) that assists in many biochemical functions needed for life

Mucosa — the innermost layer of the GI tract; the mucosa itself is made of three layers: the epithelium, the lamina propria, and the muscularis mucosae

Muscularis externa — the layer of the GI tract containing the muscles responsible for contraction and peristalsis

Nasopharynx — the superior portion of the pharynx that extends from the rear of the nasal cavity to the level of the soft palate

Nutrient — a substance in food that is used by the body to live and grow

Omentum — a large apron-like fold of the peritoneal lining that is draped over the front of the abdominal organs

Oropharynx — the portion of the pharynx from the soft palate down to the level of the hyoid bone

Pancreas — a gland located behind the stomach that secretes digestive enzymes

Pancreatitis — inflammation of the pancreas

Parietal cell — a type of cell in the stomach that secretes hydrochloric acid

Parotitis — inflammation of the parotid glands

Peristalsis — the coordinated contraction and relaxation of the muscles in the GI tract; this process moves food along the length of the GI tract

Peritoneum — the serous membrane that lines the abdominopelvic cavity

Peritonitis — inflammation of the peritoneum

Pharynx — a funnel shaped tube that extends from the back of the mouth down to the level of the larynx and the esophagus; it is often called "the throat"

Portal triad — a structure in a liver lobule consisting of a small vein, a small artery, and a bile duct

Propulsion — the movement of food along the GI tract

Proteins — substances that make up the structural components of the body, such as collagen and hair; furthermore, things like enzymes and antibodies are proteins

Saliva — a liquid secreted into the mouth by the salivary glands

Serosa — the outer connective tissue covering of the GI tract

Small intestine — the portion of the GI tract between the stomach and the large intestine; it consists of the duodenum, jejunum, and ileum

Sphincter — a ring of muscle that guards the opening at the end of a tube

Stomach — the organ in the GI tract located between the esophagus and the small intestine; it secretes acid to aid in digestion

Submucosa — connective tissue layer that supports the mucosa; it contains blood vessels and nerve fibers

Vestigial organ — term used for an organ in the body that is supposedly a useless leftover from our evolutionary past; in reality, there are no useless organs in the body

Vitamin — a type of micronutrient needed for the proper function of various biochemical processes in the body

Xerostomia — dry mouth syndrome; it is most often the result of an abnormally low production of saliva

Photo Credits

AUTHOR
DR. TOMMY MITCHELL

Dr. Tommy Mitchell graduated with a BA with highest honors from the University of Tennessee-Knoxville in 1980 with a major in cell biology. For his superior scholarship during his undergraduate study, he was elected to Phi Beta Kappa Society (the oldest and one of the most respected honor societies in America). He subsequently attended Vanderbilt University School of Medicine, where he received his medical degree in 1984.

Dr. Mitchell completed his residency at Vanderbilt University Affiliated Hospitals in 1987. He is Board Certified in Internal Medicine. In 1991, he was elected a Fellow of the American College of Physicians (F.A.C.P.). Tommy had a thriving medical practice in his hometown of Gallatin, Tennessee, for 20 years, but, in late 2006, he withdrew from medical practice to join Answers in Genesis, where he presently serves as a full time speaker, writer, and researcher.

As a scientist, physician, and father, Dr. Mitchell has a burden to provide solid answers from the Bible to equip people to stand in the face of personal tragedy and popular evolutionary misinformation. Using communication skills developed over many years of medical practice, he is able to connect with people at all educational levels and unveil the truth that can change their lives.

Dr. Mitchell has been married to his wife, Elizabeth (herself a retired obstetrician), for over 30 years; they have three daughters. His hobbies include Martin guitars, anything to do with Bill Monroe (the famous bluegrass musician), and Apple computers. He does also admit to spending an excessive amount of time playing cribbage with Ken Ham.

INDEX

Absorption............7-10, 40, 58-59, 63, 66,
.... 70, 76, 80, 84, 88, 91, 106
Accessory digestive organs 6-7, 14,
.... 16-17, 43, 106
Accessory duct................................. 45-46
Acini 46-47
Acute hepatitis 54
Adenosine diphosphate (ADP) 100
Adenosine triphosphate (ATP) ... 100, 106
Adventitia....................................... 11, 31
Aerobic respiration.............. 100-103, 106
Albumin.. 55, 80
Alimentary canal 6, 30, 106
Amino acids....................5, 54-55, 57, 63,
.... 72, 77-81, 96, 103, 106
Ampulla 45
Ampulla of Vater................................... 45
Amylase.................. 26, 28, 47, 63, 74-75
Anabolism 99, 103, 106
Anaerobic respiration.......... 100-102, 106
Appendicitis 67, 106
Appendix 7, 13, 36, 64, 67, 106
Arteries
    celiac 36, 48, 61
    gastroomental 37
    inferior mesenteric...................... 66
    inferior pancreaticoduodenal 61
    inferior phrenic 31
    inferior thyroid............................ 31
    left gastric 31, 36-37
    left gastroepiploic 36-37
    right gastric 36-37
    right gastroepiploic 36-37
    splenic 48
    superior mesenteric.......... 48, 61, 66
    superior pancreaticoduodenal...... 61
    vasa recta.......................... 61, 63, 66
Ascorbic acid 85-86, 93
Aspiration.. 33
Beriberi... 85-87
Bile 45, 48-56, 63, 84, 106-107
Bile canaliculi 50-51
Bile salts 52-54, 56, 84, 106
Bilirubin................................52-53, 55
Biotin.......................................69, 86-87
Body Mass Index (BMI)...... 92, 95, 97, 106
Bolus....................7, 13, 25, 28-29, 33-34
Burping.. 44
Calorie 92, 94, 103, 106
Carbohydrates 41, 57, 68, 71-73,
.................................75, 77, 79-81, 84,
.........90, 92, 94-97, 99, 102-103, 106
Catabolism........................... 99, 103, 106
Cellular respiration.............100, 103, 106
Cellulose...74, 91
Cementum.................................... 18-19
Ceruloplasmin 55
Chemical digestion.........................8, 106
Chief cells.................................... 37-39

Cholecystokinin......................45, 63
Cholesterol 55-57, 82-83, 91, 93-94
Chronic hepatitis 54
Chylomicrons 63, 84
Chyme 39, 57, 63, 75, 79, 106
Chymotrypsinogen 47
Circular folds 58-59, 66
Citric acid cycle 101-103
Clostridium difficile............................ 69
Colonoscopy 62, 65
Colostrum.. 80
Common bile duct 45, 49, 52-53, 56
Common hepatic duct 49, 51, 53
Complex carbohydrates ..68, 73, 75, 77, 96
Crypts of Lieberkühn 59
Dental caries............................21, 106
Dentin....................18-19, 21-22, 86
Deoxyribonuclease 47
Digestion 5, 7-8, 10, 13, 15, 18, 26, 28,
.........................32, 34, 39, 43, 52-53,
.... 55, 75, 79-80, 84, 99, 106-107
Dipeptide.. 77
Disaccharide 73, 75
Diverticula 65
Diverticular Disease............................ 65
Diverticulitis... 65
Diverticulosis....................................... 65
Duct of Santorini 45
Duodenal ulcer 42
Duodenum..........35-36, 39, 41-43, 45-48,
    52-53, 568-59, 61-63, 75, 79, 84, 107
Electron transport chain............. 101-102
Elimination.........................8, 11, 91, 106
Emulsification 63, 84
Enamel....................18-23, 25-27, 89, 106
Endocrine gland....................24, 43
Endoscope 32, 62, 106
Enteric nervous system 13, 106
Enterocytes......... 60, 63-64, 75-76, 80, 84
Enterohepatic circulation............. 54, 106
Epiglottis 29, 33
Eructation.. 44
Esophageal hiatus............................... 30
Esophagogastroduodenoscopy 62
Esophagus 6-8, 10-11, 14, 16,
................29-36, 41, 44, 60, 106-107
Essential amino acids 78, 80, 106
Essential nutrient 72, 106
Exocrine gland........................24, 43, 47
Falciform ligament 49
Fat-soluble vitamins............................ 84
Fatty acids 69, 72, 81, 83, 103, 107
Feces.......................8-9, 53, 66-67, 69, 91
Fluoride 19-20, 89
Folic acid 69, 87
G cell... 41
Gallbladder 7, 43-46, 48-49,
..............................51, 53, 56, 63, 84, 106
Gallstones 47, 56, 95

Gastric belch...................................... 44
Gastric glands 38-39
Gastric pits 38
Gastric ulcer 42
Gastrin..39, 41
Gastroenterologist............................. 62
Gastroesophageal reflux disease.......... 32
Gastrointestinal (GI) tract 6, 9, 106
Gingiva 18-19
Gingivitis 21-22, 106
Gland 24-25, 39, 43, 47-48, 67,
....89, 106-107
Gluconeogenesis................................ 57
Glycogen.............. 55, 57, 74, 99, 102, 106
Glycolysis 100-103
Goblet cells.................................60, 66
Goiter......................................89-90
Greater curvature 35-36
Greater omentum 36
Gums 15, 18-23, 86, 106
Halitosis 27, 106
Hard palate 15, 29
Haustra 65-66
Heartburn 32
Helicobacter pylori 42
Hepatic flexure 65
Hepatic laminae................................. 50
Hepatic sinusoids 50-52
Hepatitis 52, 54, 107
Hepatocyte 49-50, 107
Hepatopancreatic ampulla 45
Hiatal hernia..................................... 32
High density lipoprotein (HDL) 82
Ileocecal junction 58, 64
Immunoglobulins 25, 80
Ingestion 7, 107
Intestinal glands.................59-60, 63, 66
Intrinsic factor.....................39-40, 88
Islets of Langerhans 46-47
Jaundice 52, 54, 56
Krebs cycle.......................................101
Lactase.. 75
Lacteal 59
Lactic acid...102
Large intestine, parts of
    ascending colon.....................65, 107
    cecum 64-65, 67, 107
    descending colon...................65, 107
    rectum 65-66, 68, 107
    sigmoid colon 65, 107
    transverse colon 36, 65, 107
Laryngopharynx 29-30, 107
Left hepatic duct................................ 51
Lesser curvature 35-36
Lesser omentum 36
Lipase 26, 28, 39, 63
Lipids...................... 47, 53, 63-64, 71-72,
.... 80-81, 84, 90, 106-107
Lipogenesis............................... 102-103

wonders of the HUMAN BODY SERIES

JR. HIGH STUDENT

VOL. 1
THE MUSCULOSKELETAL SYSTEM

wonders of the HUMAN BODY

Dr. Tommy Mitchell

ISBN: 978-0-89051-865-6
Case • 8½ x 11 • 112 pages
JUVENILE NONFICTION / Science & Nature / Anatomy & Physiology
SCIENCE / Life Sciences / Human Anatomy & Physiology

JR. HIGH STUDENT

VOL. 2
CARDIOVASCULAR & RESPIRATORY SYSTEMS

wonders of the HUMAN BODY

Dr. Tommy Mitchell

ISBN: 978-0-89051-928-8
Case • 8½ x 11 • 112 pages
JUVENILE NONFICTION / Science & Nature / Anatomy & Physiology
SCIENCE / Life Sciences / Human Anatomy & Physiology

ALSO AVAILABLE
INTRODUCTION TO ANATOMY & PHYSIOLOGY

Learn about the musculoskeletal system and the cardiovascular and respiratory systems from the cell level to the systems themselves. There will be no denying that the human body can only be the product of a Master Designer.

ISBN: 978-0-89051-929-5
Paper • 8½ x 11 • 260 pages
JUVENILE NONFICTION / Science & Nature / Anatomy & Physiology
RELIGION / Christian Education / Children & Youth